STEVE

Biography

THE LIFE OF A VISIONARY

April N Mcvay

CONTENTS

CHAPTER 1

CHILDHOOD

CHAPTER 2

THE DROPOUT

CHAPTER 3

ATARI AND INDIA

CHAPTER 4

THE APPLE I

CHAPTER 5

THE APPLE II

CHAPTER 6

CHRISANN AND LISA

CHAPTER 7

THE MAC IS BORN

CHAPTER 8

ENTER SCULLEY

CHAPTER 9

ICARUS

CHAPTER 10

NeXT

CHAPTER 11

PIXAR

CHAPTER 12

THE RELATIONSHIP IS PAST

CHAPTER 13

LOCATING JOANNE AND MONA

CHAPTER 14

THE LOST FATHER

CHAPTER 15

FAMILY MAN

CHAPTER 16

LISA

CHAPTER 17

CHILDREN

CHAPTER 18

TOY STORY

CHAPTER 19

THE SECOND COMING

CHAPTER 20

REVIVAL

CHAPTER 21

CANCER

CHAPTER 22

EVOLUTION

CHAPTER 23

THE CANCER RECURS

CHAPTER 24

THE iPAD

CHAPTER 25

NEW BATTLES

CHAPTER 26

TO INFINITY

CHAPTER 27

ROUND THREE

CHAPTER 1

CHILDHOOD

Paul Reinhold Jobs grew up on a dairy farm outside Germantown, Wisconsin. Despite the fact that his father was an alcoholic and occasionally harsh, Paul developed a peaceful and calm demeanour beneath his leathery skin. After dropping out of high school, he roamed through the Midwest working as a mechanic until, at the age of nineteen, he joined the Coast Guard despite not knowing how to swim. He was assigned to the USS General M. C. Meigs spent most of the war ferrying troops to Italy for General Patton. His abilities as a machinist and fireman garnered him praise, although he was periodically involved in small mishaps and never promoted above the rank of sailor. Clara was born in New Jersey, where her parents had fled the Turks in Armenia, and her family later relocated to San Francisco's Mission District when she was a toddler. She kept a secret from everyone: she had previously been married, but her husband had been killed in the war. So when she met Paul Jobs on that first date, she was ready to embark on a new adventure.

Joanne travelled to Syria with Abdulfattah in the summer of 1954. They spent two months in Homs, where she learnt to prepare Syrian delicacies from his family. She realised she was pregnant when they returned to Wisconsin. They were both twenty-three years old when they chose not to marry. At the time, her father was dying, and he had threatened to disown her if she married Abdulfattah. Abortion was also not an easy choice in a tiny Catholic town. So Joanne moved to San Francisco in early 1955, where she was taken into the care of a sympathetic doctor who harboured unwed mothers, delivered their kids, and surreptitiously arranged closed adoptions. Joanne stipulated that her child be adopted by college graduates. As a result, the doctor made arrangements for the kid to be put with a lawyer and his wife. But when a boy was born on February 24, 1955, the intended pair changed their minds and opted for a daughter. As a result, the boy became the son of a high school dropout with a passion for mechanics and his down-to-earth wife who worked as an accountant, rather than a lawyer. Clara and Paul called their infant son Steven Paul Jobs. Joanne refused to sign the adoption paperwork after learning that her kid had been placed with a couple who had not even completed high school. Even after the baby had adjusted into the Jobs household, the standoff lasted weeks. Joanne eventually agreed, but only on the condition that the couple promise—indeed, make a pledge—to finance a savings account to pay for the boy's college education.

There was another reason Joanne was hesitant to sign the adoption paperwork. Her father was dying, and she intended to marry Jandali soon after. She hoped, she would later tell family members, often crying at the memory, that after they were married, she would be able to reclaim their baby boy. After the adoption was finalised, Arthur Schieble died in August 1955. Joanne and Abdulfattah married in Green Bay's St. Philip the Apostle Catholic Church just after Christmas that year. The next year, he received his PhD in international politics, and they welcomed their second child, a girl called Mona. After her divorce from Jandali in 1962, Joanne began a dreamlike and peripatetic life that her daughter, the great novelist Mona Simpson, would describe in her book Anywhere but Here. Because Steve's adoption had been finalised, it would take them twenty years to find each other.

Steve Jobs was aware of his adoption from a young age. "My parents were very open with me about that," he said. He remembered sitting on his front lawn when he was six or seven years old, telling the girl who lived across the way. "So does that mean your real parents didn't want you?" the girl inquired. "Lightning bolts went off in my head," Jobs said. "I remember crying and running into the house." And my parents told me, 'No, you have to understand.' They took me seriously and looked me in the eyes. 'We intentionally chose you,' they said. My parents both stated it and repeated it gently for me. And they emphasised each word in that sentence."

In many ways, the upbringing that Paul and Clara Jobs built for their new son was a late 1950s caricature. They adopted a daughter called Patty when Steve was two years old, and three years later they moved to a tract house in the suburbs. CIT, the finance firm where Paul worked as a repo man, had transferred him to its Palo Alto office, but he couldn't afford to live there, so they settled in a neighbourhood in Mountain View, a less costly town just to the south. There, Paul attempted to pass on his passion for mechanics and automobiles. "Steve, this is your workbench now," he remarked, marking off a section of their garage table. Jobs recalled being struck by his father's attention to detail. "I thought my dad's sense of design was pretty good," he added, "because he could build anything." He would build us a cabinet if we needed one. He gave me a hammer so I could help him build our fence."

The fence still surrounds the back and side yards of the Mountain View house fifty years later. Jobs caressed the stockade panels as he showed it to me, recalling a lesson his father instilled in him. Even though the backs of cupboards and fences were unseen, his father stressed the need of correctly crafting them. "He was obsessed with doing things correctly. He was even concerned with the appearance of the sections you couldn't see."

His father kept restoring and reselling used cars, and he decorated the garage with photos of his favourites. He would point out the design's details to his son: the lines, the vents, the chrome, the seat trim. Every day after work, he changed into his dungarees and went to the garage, often accompanied by Steve. "I figured I could get him nailed down with a little mechanical ability, but he really wasn't interested in getting his hands dirty," Paul later remembered. "He was never particularly interested in mechanical things."

"I wasn't all that into fixing cars," Jobs said. "However, I was eager to see my father." Even as he became more conscious that he had been adopted, he became closer to his father. He discovered a photograph of his father from his stint in the Coast Guard when he was about eight years old. "He's in the engine room, shirtless and looking like James Dean." For a child, it was one of those "Oh wow" moments. Wow, yeah, my parents were once extremely youthful and really attractive."

Steve's father introduced him to electronics through automobiles. "My father didn't know much about electronics, but he'd seen it a lot in automobiles and other things he fixed." He introduced me to the fundamentals of electronics, which piqued my curiosity." The travels to scavenge for parts were much more fascinating. "Every weekend, we'd go junkyarding. We'd be looking for a generator, a carburetor, and other parts." He remembers seeing his father bargain at the counter. "He was a good bargainer because he knew what the parts should cost better than the guys at the counter." This contributed to his parents' vow when he was adopted. "My college fund came from my father paying $50 for a beat-up car that didn't run, working on it for a few weeks, and selling it for $250—all while not telling the IRS."

CHAPTER 2

THE DROPOUT

Jobs began dating a girl called Chrisann Brennan, who was about his age but still a junior, near the conclusion of his senior year at Homestead in the spring of 1972. She was quite gorgeous, with her light brown hair, green eyes, high cheekbones, and fragile aura. She was also dealing with the dissolution of her parents' marriage, which made her vulnerable. "We worked together on an animated movie, then we started going out, and she became my first real girlfriend," Jobs remembered. "Steve was kind of crazy," Brennan subsequently said. That is why I was drawn to him." After graduating, he and Brennan relocated to a cabin in the hills above Los Altos that summer. "I'm going to live in a cabin with Chrisann," he said one day to his parents. His father was enraged. "No, you're not," he replied. "Over my dead body." They had lately clashed over marijuana, and the younger Jobs was once again stubborn. He simply said goodbye and walked away. When Jobs was adopted, his parents promised him that he would attend college. So they worked hard and diligently for his college money, which was modest but sufficient by the time he graduated. But Jobs, who was getting increasingly obstinate, made it difficult. He considered not attending college at all at first. "I think I would have gone to New York if I hadn't gone to college," he reflected, pondering how different his world—and probably all of ours—might have been if he hadn't gone to college. When his parents urged him to attend college, he reacted passive-aggressively. Despite the fact that state schools, such as Berkeley, where Woz was at the time, were more economical, he did not consider them. He also didn't consider Stanford, which was just up the road and was likely to give a scholarship. "The kids who went to Stanford, they already knew what they wanted to do," he explained. "They weren't really artistic. "I wanted something more artistic and intriguing."

Instead, he insisted on only applying to Reed College, a private liberal arts college in Portland, Oregon, and one of the most costly in the country. He was in Berkeley visiting Woz when his father called to announce an admission letter from Reed had arrived, and he tried to talk Steve out of coming. His mother felt the same way. They claimed it was way beyond their means. Their son, on the other hand, issued an ultimatum: if he couldn't go to Reed, he wouldn't go anywhere. As usual, they caved. When it came time for Jobs to matriculate in the fall of 1972, his parents took him up to Portland, but he refused to let them on campus in another minor act of rebellion. In fact, he didn't even say goodbye or thank you. Later, he reflected on the incident with unusual regret. Jobs grew fast bored with college. He enjoyed Reed, but he didn't take the requisite classes. In fact, he was astonished to learn that, despite the hippy vibe, there were severe course requirements. Jobs subsequently admitted that he began to feel bad about spending so much of his parents' money on an education that did not appear to be valuable. "All of my working-class parents' savings were being spent on my college tuition," he explained in a famous Stanford commencement speech. "I didn't know what I wanted to do with my life and had no idea how college would help me figure it out." And here I was, blowing through all of the money my parents had saved their entire lives. So I chose to drop out and trust that everything will be fine." He didn't want to leave Reed; he just didn't want to pay tuition and take subjects that didn't interest him. Reed, surprisingly, tolerated it. "He had a very inquiring mind that was enormously attractive," stated Jack Dudman, dean of students. "He refused to accept automatically received truths, and he wanted to examine everything for himself." Even when Jobs stopped paying tuition, Dudman enabled him to audit classes and stay in the dorms with pals.

CHAPTER 3

ATARI AND INDIA

After eighteen months of hanging out with Reed, Jobs decided to return to his parents' house in Los Altos and hunt for work. Nolan Bushnell, the burly entrepreneur who founded Atari, was a captivating visionary with a wonderful touch of showmanship in him—in other words, another role model begging to be mimicked. Alcorn was summoned when Jobs arrived in the Atari lobby wearing sandals and demanded a job. "'We've got a hippie youngster in the foyer,' I was told. He claims he will not go unless we hire him. Is it better to call the cops or let him in?' "Bring him in!" I said. Jobs was thus one of Atari's initial fifty employees, working as a technician for $5 an hour. "Hiring a Reed dropout was strange in retrospect," Alcorn remarked. "But I noticed something in him. He was incredibly intelligent, passionate, and enthusiastic about technology."

Jobs was eager to generate money in early 1974 because Robert Friedland, who had visited India the previous summer, was pressing him to go on his own spiritual journey there. When Jobs informed Atari that he was leaving to seek a guru in India, the cheerful Alcorn was amused. "He comes in and stares at me and declares, 'I'm going to find my guru,' and I say, 'No shit, that's super. 'Please contact me!' And when he claims he wants me to help pay, I say, 'Bullshit!'" Then Alcorn had a thought. Atari was producing kits and shipping them to Munich, where they were assembled into final devices and supplied by a Turin wholesaler. But there was a catch: because the games were developed for the American frame rate of sixty frames per second, there were frustrating interference issues in Europe, where the frame rate was fifty frames per second. Alcorn devised a solution with Jobs and then offered to pay for him to travel to Europe to put it into action. "It's gotta be cheaper to get to India from there," he reasoned. Jobs concurred. So Alcorn sent him out with the instruction, "Say hello to your guru for me."

Jobs returned to New Delhi to meet Daniel Kottke, who arrived in India at the start of the summer. They wandered aimlessly, mostly by bus. Jobs was no longer looking for a guru to give wisdom; instead, he was pursuing enlightenment via ascetic experience, deprivation, and simplicity. He was unable to acquire inner peace. Kottke recalls

Jobs getting into a heated argument with a Hindu woman at a small bazaar who, Jobs claimed, was diluting down the milk she was selling them. Jobs, on the other hand, might be generous. When they arrived in Manali, Kottke's sleeping bag was stolen, along with his traveller's checks. "Steve covered my food expenses and bus ticket back to Delhi," Kottke said. He also gave Kottke $100 of his own money to tide him through. He had only written to his parents irregularly during his seven months in India, receiving letters at the American Express office in New Delhi when he went through, so they were taken aback when they received a call from the Oakland airport asking them to pick him up. They drove up from Los Altos right away. "My head had been shaved, I was wearing Indian cotton robes, and my skin had turned a deep, chocolate brown-red from the sun," he remembered. "So I'm sitting there and my parents walked past me about five times before my mother came up to me and asked, 'Steve?' and I said, 'Hi!'"

They returned him to his home, where he began his search for himself. It was a quest with numerous paths to enlightenment. He would meditate and study Zen in the mornings and evenings, and in between he would attend physics or engineering classes at Stanford. Jobs' interest in Eastern mysticism, Hinduism, Zen Buddhism, and the quest for enlightenment was not a passing fad for a teen. Throughout his life, he would strive to follow many of the fundamental principles of Eastern faiths, such as the emphasis on experiencing praj knowledge or cognitive comprehension that is instinctively realised through mental concentration. Years later, as he sat in his Palo Alto garden, he mused on the long-term impact of his journey to India.

Coming back to America was a much bigger cultural shock for me than travelling to India. People in the Indian countryside do not use their brain like we do; instead, they use their intuition, which is significantly more developed than in the rest of the world. Intuition is a very powerful thing, in my opinion more powerful than intelligence. That has had a significant impact on my job.

Western logical mind is not an intrinsic human quality; it is learnt, and it is Western civilization's greatest achievement. They never learned it in India's countryside. They learnt something else, which is valuable in some ways but not in others. That is the power of intuition and experience.

Al Alcorn was sitting in his office at Atari in early 1975 when Ron Wayne walked in. He exclaimed, "Hey, Stevie is back!"

"Wow, bring him in," Alcorn responded.

Jobs shuffled in barefoot, wearing a saffron robe and clutching a copy of Be Here Now, which he insisted Alcorn read. "Can I have my job back?" he inquired.

"He looked like a Hare Krishna guy, but it was great to see him," Alcorn said. "So I said, sure!"

Jobs worked largely at night for the purpose of harmony once more. One day in the late summer of 1975, Nolan Bushnell decided to create a single-player version of Pong, contradicting the popular belief that paddle games were dead. Instead of competing against an opponent, the player would volley the ball into a wall that lost a brick anytime it was struck. He summoned Jobs to his office, drew it on his small chalkboard, and requested him to design it. Bushnell told him there would be a bonus for every chip he used that was less than fifty. Bushnell was aware that Jobs was not a terrific engineer, but he rightly expected that he would hire Wozniak, who was usually hanging around. "I looked at it as a two-for-one thing," Bushnell said. "Woz was the better engineer."

Wozniak was overjoyed when Jobs asked him to assist and suggested dividing the fee. Surprisingly, they completed the task in four days, with Wozniak using only forty-five chips. Recollections vary, although by all accounts Jobs just gave Wozniak half of his normal salary rather than the extra Bushnell received for salvaging five chips. It would be another ten years before Wozniak learnt (via a story in an Atari history book named Zap) that Jobs had been awarded this bonus.

CHAPTER 4

THE APPLE I

The club was dubbed the Homebrew Computer Club, and it embodied the Whole Earth combination of counterculture and technology. It would become something close to what the Turk's Head café was to the Dr. Johnson era, a location where ideas were exchanged and spread. The flyer for the inaugural meeting, held on March 5, 1975, in French's Menlo Park garage, was written by Moore: "Are you creating your own computer? It inquired, "Terminal, TV, typewriter?" "If that's the case, you might want to attend a gathering of people who share your interests."

When Allen Baum saw the flyer on the HP bulletin board, he called Wozniak, who agreed to accompany him. "That turned out to be one of the most important nights of my life," Wozniak said. About thirty more individuals arrived, spilling out of French's open garage door, and took turns discussing their hobbies. According to the minutes made by Moore, Wozniak said he preferred "video games, pay movies for hotels, scientific calculator design, and TV terminal design," and subsequently admitted to being quite frightened. There was a demonstration of the new Altair, but viewing the specification sheet for a CPU was more essential to Wozniak. He had an epiphany while thinking about the microprocessor—a chip that included a full central processing unit. He was working on a terminal with a keyboard and monitor that would link to a remote minicomputer. Using a microprocessor, he could place some of the minicomputer's capacity inside the terminal itself, transforming it into a small stand-alone computer on a desktop. It was a timeless concept: a keyboard, screen, and computer in one integrated personal box. "This whole vision of a personal computer just kind of popped into my head," he explained. "That night, I began to doodle on paper what would later be known as the Apple I."

Initially, he intended to use the same CPU as in the Altair, an Intel 8080. But because each of those "cost almost as much as my monthly rent," he sought an alternative. He discovered one in a Motorola 6800, which a friend at HP was able to obtain for $40 each. Then he discovered a chip made by MOS Technologies that was identical on the inside but only cost $20. It would make his machine more economical, but at a long-term cost. Intel's chips eventually became the industry standard, which would come back to harm Apple when its computers were incompatible with them. Every day after work, Wozniak would head home for a TV meal before returning to HP to work on his computer. He laid out the parts in his cubicle, worked out where they should go, and soldered them to his motherboard. Then he started building software to get the CPU to display images on the screen. He developed the code by hand because he couldn't afford to pay for computer time. After a few months, he was ready to put it to the test. "I was shocked when I typed a few keys on the keyboard!" The letters appeared on the screen." It was Sunday, June 29, 1975, and it was a watershed moment for the personal computer. "It was the first time in history," Wozniak later explained, "anyone had typed a character on a keyboard and seen it show up on their own computer's screen right in front of them."

Jobs was blown away. He peppered Wozniak with questions, including if the computer might ever be networked. Could a disk for memory storage be added? He also began assisting Woz in obtaining components. The dynamic random-access memory chips were very crucial. Jobs made a few phone calls and was able to get some free from Intel. "Steve is exactly that kind of person," Wozniak remarked. "I mean, he knew how to talk to a salesperson." That is something I could never accomplish. I'm far too shy."

Woz was usually too nervous to speak up at meetings, but afterward, everyone would gather around his machine, and he would proudly show off his progress. Moore had attempted to inculcate an ethos of exchanging and sharing rather than commerce in the Homebrew. "The theme of the club," Woz explained, "was Give to help others.'" It exemplified the hacker ethic of information freedom and distrust of any authority. "I designed the Apple I because I wanted to give it away for free to other people," Wozniak explained.

Bill Gates did not share this viewpoint. After he and Paul Allen finished their BASIC interpreter for the Altair, Gates was outraged to discover that members of the Homebrew were making copies and sharing them without paying him. So he wrote the club what would become a famous letter: "As the majority of hobbyists must be aware, the majority of you steal your software." Is this correct?... You do one thing: you prevent good software from being written. Who can afford to do expert work for free?... I'd appreciate letters from anyone willing to pay."

Similarly, Steve Jobs rejected the concept that Wozniak's products, whether a Blue Box or a computer, desired to be free. As a result, he persuaded Wozniak to cease handing away copies of his schematics. Jobs contended that most users didn't have the time to develop it themselves. "Why don't we build and sell printed circuit boards to them?" It was an illustration of their symbiotic relationship. Wozniak sold his HP 65 calculator for $500 to raise the funds they required, but the buyer only paid him half of that. Jobs, for one, sold his Volkswagen bus for $1,500. However, the buyer returned two weeks later to inform Jobs that the engine had failed, and Jobs agreed to pay for half of the repairs. Despite these minor failures, they now had approximately $1,300 in working cash, a product design, and a plan, with their own tiny savings tossed in. They intended to establish their own computer company. Jobs ' home in Los Altos was transformed into an assembly facility for the fifty Apple Iboard that had to be delivered to the Byte Shop within thirty days, when the payment for the parts was due. Jobs and Wozniak were joined by Daniel Kottke, his ex-girlfriend Elizabeth Holmes (who had left the cult she had joined), and Jobs' pregnant sister, Patty. Her vacant bedroom, kitchen table, and garage were all commandeered as work spaces. Paul Jobs put his side business of restoring old vehicles on hold so that the Apple crew could utilise the entire garage.

Apple was on the edge of profitability after thirty days. "Because I got a good deal on parts, we were able to build the boards for less than we thought," Jobs recounted. "So the fifty we sold to the Byte Shop paid for almost all of the material we needed to make a hundred boards." They might now make a substantial profit by selling the remaining fifty to their friends and fellow Homebrew enthusiasts.

CHAPTER 5

THE APPLE II

The release of the Apple II was timed to coincide with the first West Coast Computer Faire, which was to be held in April 1977 in San Francisco and was coordinated by Homebrew stalwart Jim Warren. As soon as he received the information packet, Jobs signed Apple up for a booth. He wanted to secure a prominent location near the entrance to the hall as a spectacular way to unveil the Apple II, so he surprised Wozniak by paying $5,000 in advance. "Steve decided that this was going to be our big launch," Wozniak explained. "We would show the world that we had a great machine and a great company."

The work was well worth it. In contrast to the scary metal-clad machines and naked boards on the other tables, the Apple II appeared sturdy yet inviting in its elegant beige housing. At the event, Apple received 300 orders, and Jobs met Mizushima Satoshi, a Japanese textile manufacturer who became Apple's first reseller in Japan. Apple was now a real firm, with a dozen workers, a credit line, and the daily pressures that customers and suppliers can bring. It had even moved out of the Jobses' garage and into a rented office on Stevens Creek Boulevard in Cupertino, about a mile from the high school that Jobs and Wozniak had attended.

Jobs did not gracefully accept his increasing responsibilities. He had always been volatile and obnoxious. His actions had landed him on the night shift at Atari, but this was not an option at Apple.

Jobs' demeanour irritated Wozniak. "Steve was far too harsh on individuals. "I wanted our company to feel like a family, where we could all have fun and share whatever we created." Jobs, for one, believed that Wozniak would never mature. "He had a childlike demeanour. He wrote a terrific version of BASIC but never got around to writing the floating-point BASIC we needed, so we had to make a deal with Microsoft later on. He was simply too disinterested."

However, for the time being, the personality clashes were bearable, owing to the company's success.

CHAPTER 6

CHRISANN AND LISA

Chrisann Brennan has been in and out of Jobs' life since they lived together in a cabin the summer after he graduated from high school. They spent time together at Robert Friedland's estate after he returned from India in 1974. "Steve invited me up there, and we were just young, easy, and free," she remembered. "There was an energy there that went straight to my heart."

When they returned to Los Altos, their relationship deteriorated to the point where it was mostly friendly. He lived at home and worked at Atari; she had a little apartment and spent a lot of time at the Zen centre run by Kobun Chino. By early 1975, she had started dating a mutual acquaintance, Greg Calhoun. According to Elizabeth Holmes, "she was with Greg but occasionally went back to Steve." "That was pretty much the case for all of us. We were shifting back and forth; it was the 1970s, after all."

Calhoun worked at Reed alongside Jobs, Friedland, Kottke, and Holmes. He, like the others, became seriously immersed in Eastern mysticism, dropped out of Reed, and eventually ended up at Friedland's farm. He relocated to an eight-by-twenty-foot chicken coop, which he turned into a small house by lifting it on cinder blocks and constructing a sleeping loft inside. Brennan moved in with him in the spring of 1975, and the following year they decided to make their own trip to India. Jobs told Calhoun not to bring Brennan because she would interfere with his spiritual journey, but they went regardless. "I was just so impressed by what happened to Steve on his trip to India that I wanted to go there," she explained.

Their journey, which began in March 1976 and lasted over a year, was serious. They ran out of money at one point, so Calhoun hitchhiked to Iran to teach English in Tehran. Brennan remained in India, and when Calhoun's teaching assignment ended, they hitchhiked to meet in the middle, in Afghanistan. Back then, the world was a totally different place. Their relationship deteriorated over time, and they returned from India separately. Brennan had returned to Los Altos by the summer of 1977, when she stayed in a tent on the grounds of Kobun Chino's Zen centre. Jobs had moved out of his parents' house by this point and was living with Daniel Kottke in a $600-per-month suburban ranch house in Cupertino. It was a strange scene of free-spirited hippy types living in Rancho Suburbia, a tract house. "It was a four-bedroom house, and we occasionally rented out one of the bedrooms to all sorts of crazy people, including a stripper for a while," Jobs remembered. Kottke couldn't figure out why Jobs hadn't purchased his own house by then, which he could have afforded. "I think he just wanted to have a roommate," hypothesised Kottke. Despite her inconsistent relationship with Jobs, Brennan soon moved in with her. This resulted in a living situation worthy of a French farce. The house included two large bedrooms and two little bedrooms. Jobs, predictably, took over the larger of them, and Brennan (who was not actually living with him) went into the second enormous bedroom. "The two middle rooms were like for babies, and I didn't want either of them, so I moved into the living room and slept on a foam pad," Kottke explained. They converted one of the small rooms into a meditative and acid-dropping place, similar to the attic one they had used at Reed. It was stuffed with packing foam from Apple boxes. "Neighbourhood kids used to come over and we would toss them in it, and it was great fun," Kottke explained, "but then Chrisann brought home some cats who peed in the foam, and we had to get rid of it."

Brennan and Jobs' intimate relationship was renewed by living in the house at times, and she became pregnant within a few months. "Steve and I were in and out of a relationship for about five years before I got pregnant," she explained. "We didn't know how to be together and how to be apart." On Thanksgiving 1977, when Greg Calhoun hitchhiked from Colorado to see them, Brennan broke the news: "Steve and I got back together, and now I'm pregnant, but we're on and off again, and I don't know what to do."

Calhoun saw that Jobs seemed detached from the issue. He even attempted to persuade Calhoun to stay with them and work at Apple. "Steve was just not dealing with Chrisann or the pregnancy," he said. "He could be very engaged with you one moment and then very disengaged the next." There was a shockingly chilly side to him."

When Jobs didn't want to deal with a distraction, he would sometimes simply ignore it, as if he could. He was capable of distorting reality not only for others but also for himself at times. In the event of Brennan's pregnancy, he simply ignored it. When confronted, he would deny knowing he was the father, even though he confessed sleeping with her. "I wasn't sure it was my kid because I knew I wasn't the only one she was sleeping with," he subsequently explained. "She and I weren't even dating when she got pregnant." She only needed a room in our house." Brennan was certain that Jobs was the father. She had no romantic relationships with Greg or any other guys at the time.

Was he delusory, or did he not realise he was the father? "I just think he couldn't access that part of his brain or the idea of being responsible," said Kottke. "He considered the option of parenthood and the option of not being a parent, and he decided to believe the latter," Elizabeth Holmes concurred. He had alternative ideas about his life."

There was no talk of marriage. "I knew she wasn't the person I wanted to marry, and we'd never be happy, and it wouldn't last long," Jobs stated afterwards. "I was completely in favour of her having an abortion, but she was at a loss for what to do." She considered it several times and decided not to, or I don't think she ever truly decided—I think time decided for her." Brennan informed me that having the baby was her decision: "He said he was fine with an abortion but never pushed for it." Surprisingly, considering his background, he was fiercely opposed to one option. "He strongly discouraged me from putting the child up for adoption," she explained. There was an unsettling irony. Jobs and Brennan were both twenty-three years old, the same age as Joanne Schieble and Abdulfattah Jandali when they had Jobs. He hadn't found his biological parents yet, but his adoptive parents had given him some of their story. "I didn't know about our age coincidence at the time, so it didn't affect my discussions with Chrisann," he subsequently explained. He denied that he was following in his biological father's footsteps by getting his fiancée pregnant at the age of twenty-three, but he did confess that the ironic resonance gave him pause. "Whoa!" I thought when I found out he was twenty-three when he got Joanne pregnant with me. Jobs and Brennan's relationship gradually worsened. "Chrisann would go into this victim mode, saying that Steve and I were ganging up on her," Kottke claimed. "Steve would just laugh at her and not take her seriously." Brennan was not emotionally stable, as she later revealed. She started breaking plates and throwing stuff around. Jobs, she claimed, continued to irritate her with his callousness: "He was an enlightened being who was cruel." Kottke was caught in the crossfire. "Daniel didn't have that DNA of ruthlessness, so he was a bit flipped by Steve's behaviour," Brennan says. "He would go from 'Steve's not treating you right' to laughing at me with Steve."

Robert Friedland stepped in to help her. "When he found out I was pregnant, he told me to come up to the farm and have the baby," she claimed. "So I did." Elizabeth Holmes and other friends remained in the area, and they hired an Oregon midwife to assist with the delivery. Brennan gave birth to a daughter on May 17, 1978. Jobs flew up three days later to be with them and help name the new baby. On the commune, children were given Eastern spiritual names, but Jobs insisted that she had been born in America and deserved a name that fit. Brennan concurred. They gave her the name Lisa Nicole Brennan instead of Jobs. He then departed to return to work at Apple. "He didn't want to have anything to do with her or me," Brennan explained.

She and Lisa moved into a little, decaying house in the back of a Menlo Park mansion. Brennan did not want to sue for child support, so they lived on welfare. Finally, the County of San Mateo sued Jobs in an attempt to establish paternity and force him to accept financial obligation. Jobs was initially adamant about fighting the matter. His attorneys wanted Kottke to testify that he had never seen them in bed together, and they attempted to gather evidence that Brennan had slept with other men. "At one point on the phone, I yelled at Steve, 'You know that is not true,'" Brennan remembered. "He was going to drag me through court with a little baby, trying to prove I was a whore and that anyone could have been the father of that baby."

Jobs decided to take a paternity test a year after Lisa was born. Brennan's family was taken aback, but Jobs knew Apple was about to go public and believed it was best to have the situation fixed. Jobs' DNA test was the first of its kind, and it was performed at UCLA. "I had read about DNA testing, and I was happy to do it to get things settled," he explained. The findings were largely conclusive. "The probability of paternity... is 94.41%," according to the report. Jobs was ordered by the California courts to begin paying $385 per month in child support, sign an agreement acknowledging paternity, and repay the county $5,856 in retroactive welfare payments. He was granted visitation rights but did not use them for a long period.

Jobs continued to distort reality around him even then. "He finally told us on the board," Arthur Rock said, "but he insisted that there was a good chance he wasn't the father." He was delusory." He told Time writer Michael Moritz that when the figures were crunched, it was evident that "28% of the male population in the United States could be the father." It was not merely a false claim, but also an unusual one. Worse, when Chrisann Brennan later heard what he said, she mistook Jobs' assertion for hyperbole, believing she had slept with 28% of males in the United States. "He was trying to paint me as a slut or a whore," she said. "He projected the whore image onto me in order to avoid responsibility."

Years later, Jobs expressed regret over his actions, saying, one of the few times in his life, "I wish I had handled it differently." I couldn't envision myself as a father at the time, so I avoided it. But it's not true that I was sceptical when the test results revealed she was my daughter. I agreed to support her until she was eighteen and to give Chrisann some money as well. I found a house in Palo Alto, fixed it up, and let them live there for free. Her mother chose excellent schools for her, which I paid for. I made an effort to do the right thing. But if I could do it all over again, I would.

After the matter was settled, Jobs proceeded to go on with his life, maturing in some ways but not all. He gave up drugs, relaxed his rigorous veganism, and reduced his time spent on Zen retreats. He started getting fashionable haircuts and shopping for suits and shirts at the expensive San Francisco haberdashery Wilkes Bashford. And he started dating one of Regis McKenna's staff, a stunning Polynesian-Polish woman named Barbara Jasinski. To be sure, he still had a childish rebellious element about him. He, Jasinski, and Kottke enjoyed skinny-dipping in Felt Lake on the outside of Interstate 280 near Stanford, and he purchased a 1966 BMW R60/2 motorcycle with orange tassels on the handlebars. He may still be a brat. He made fun of waitresses and frequently returned meals with the remark, "garbage." He dressed up like Jesus Christ for the company's first Halloween party in 1979, an effort of semi-ironic self-awareness that he thought was humorous but drew a lot of eye rolls. Even his first stirrings of domesticity were odd. He purchased a nice house in the Los Gatos hills and furnished it with a Maxfield Parrish painting, a Braun coffee maker, and Henckels knives. However, because he was so picky about furniture, it remained mostly empty, with no mattresses, chairs, or couches. Instead, he had a mattress in the centre of his bedroom, framed portraits of Einstein and Maharaj-ji on the walls, and an Apple II on the floor.

CHAPTER 7

THE MAC IS BORN

Jobs' key criterion for hiring people to join his merry band of pirates in the spring of 1981 was that they had a passion for the product. He would occasionally invite applicants into a room where a prototype of the Mac was draped in a fabric, dramatically reveal it, and have them watch. "If their eyes lit up, if they went right for the mouse and started pointing and clicking, Steve would smile and hire them," Andrea Cunningham remembered. "He wanted them to say,'Wow!'"

Bruce Horn worked as a programmer at Xerox PARC. Horn pondered joining the Macintosh group when some of his pals, such as Larry Tesler, opted to do so. However, he received an excellent offer with a $15,000 signing bonus to join another company. On a Friday night, Jobs called. "You have to come into Apple first thing tomorrow morning," he continued. "I have lots of stuff to show you." Horn did, and Jobs had him hooked. "Steve was so passionate about building this amazing device that would change the world," Horn said. "By the sheer force of his personality, he changed my mind." Jobs demonstrated to Horn how the plastic would be formed and put together at ideal angles, as well as how wonderful the board would appear on the inside. "He wanted me to see that this whole thing was planned out from beginning to end." Wow, I thought, I don't see that type of zeal every day. So I registered."

Jobs even attempted to re-employ Wozniak. "I resented the fact that he hadn't been doing much, but then I realised, hell, I wouldn't be here if it hadn't been for his brilliance," Jobs later told me. However, just as Jobs was beginning to pique Wozniak's interest in the Mac, he crashed his new single-engine Beechcraft while trying a takeoff near Santa Cruz. He narrowly made it and was left with partial amnesia. Jobs spent some time in the hospital, but after Wozniak recovered, he felt it was time to leave Apple. Ten years after dropping out, he decided to return to Berkeley to finish his degree, enrolling as Rocky Raccoon Clark. Jobs determined that the project should no longer be code-named after Raskin's favourite apple in order to make it his own. By early 1981, the Mac team had grown to over twenty people, and Jobs felt that they needed larger accommodations. So he relocated everyone to the second floor of a two-story brown-shingled structure roughly three blocks from Apple's headquarters. Because it was near to a Texaco station, it was dubbed Texaco Towers. He instructed the crew to purchase a sound system to make the office more vibrant. "Burrell and I ran out and bought a silver, cassette-based boombox right away, before he could change his mind," Hertzfeld remembered.

Jobs' victory was soon complete. He helped force out Mike Scott as Apple's president just a few weeks after winning his power battle with Raskin to manage the Mac division. Scotty's behaviour had become increasingly unstable, alternately aggressive and comforting. He eventually lost most of his staff support when he startled them with a series of layoffs that he handled with unusual harshness. In addition, he had developed a number of ailments, ranging from eye infections to narcolepsy. While Scott was on vacation in Hawaii, Markkula gathered the senior executives to ask if he should be replaced. The majority of them, including Jobs and John Couch, agreed. So Markkula took over as an interim and fairly inactive president, and Jobs discovered that he suddenly had complete control over the Mac division.

CHAPTER 8

ENTER SCULLEY

Mike Markkula has never aspired to be Apple's CEO. He enjoyed designing new homes, flying his private plane, and living off stock options; he did not enjoy resolving disagreement or nurturing high-maintenance egos. He had taken on the post reluctantly after feeling forced to ease Mike Scott out, and he had promised his wife that it would be a temporary one. After nearly two years, she gave him an order at the end of 1982: find a successor immediately. Jobs realised he wasn't ready to lead the company on his own, even if a part of him wanted to. He might be self-aware despite his attitude. Markkula concurred, telling Jobs that he was still a little rough-hewn and immature to be Apple's CEO. So they started looking for someone from the outside. So Jobs and Markkula hired gregarious corporate headhunter Gerry Roche to find someone else. They chose against focusing on technology leaders; instead, they required a consumer marketer who understood advertising and had the business savvy to play well on Wall Street. Roche set his eyes on the hottest consumer marketing genius of the moment, John Sculley, head of PepsiCo's Pepsi-Cola business, whose Pepsi Challenge campaign had been a commercial and public relations success. When Jobs gave a talk to Stanford business students, he had heard positive things about Sculley, who had previously talked to the class. So he told Roche that he would be delighted to meet him.

Apple's basic offices and laid-back demeanour surprised Sculley. "Most people were dressed less formally than PepsiCo's maintenance staff," he noted. During lunch, Jobs ate his salad calmly, but when Sculley said that most CEOs thought computers were more trouble than they were worth, he went into evangelical mode. "We want to change the way people use computers," he explained.

On the plane ride home, Sculley jotted down his thoughts. The final product was an eight-page study on computer marketing to consumers and corporate executives. With underlined sentences, graphs, and boxes, it was a touch sophomoric at times, but it displayed his newfound zest for figuring out how to advertise something other than Coke. "Invest in in-store merchandising that romances the consumer with Apple's potential to enrich their life!" he suggests. He was still apprehensive about leaving Pepsi, but Jobs aroused his attention. "I was taken by this young, impetuous genius and thought it would be fun to get to know him a little better," he said. So Sculley agreed to meet again when Jobs returned to New York for the debut of Lisa at the Carlyle Hotel in January 1983. The Apple team was surprised to see an unannounced visitor enter the room after a long day of press briefings. Jobs unfastened his tie and introduced Sculley as Pepsi's president and a potential huge corporate customer. Jobs chimed in with bursts of criticism sprinkled with his favourite words, "revolutionary" and "incredible," implying that the Lisa will change the nature of human interaction with computers.

CHAPTER 9

ICARUS

The introduction of the Macintosh in January 1984 catapulted Jobs into even greater celebrity. His status was restored at Apple. Instead of attempting to limit Jobs' authority, Sculley increased it: With Jobs in command, the Lisa and Macintosh departments were merged. He was flying high, yet this did not make him more relaxed. Indeed, his ruthless honesty was on display when he stood in front of the united Lisa and Macintosh teams to outline how they would be integrated. He stated that his Macintosh group leaders would be given all of the top posts, and that a fourth of the Lisa workforce would be put off. "You guys failed," he remarked directly to those who worked on the Lisa. "You're on the B team. B-team players. Too many employees here are B or C players, therefore we're releasing some of you today to work at our sister companies in the valley."

Jobs and Sculley were able to convince themselves that their friendship was still solid for the time being. They were so enthusiastic about each other that they sounded like high school sweethearts at a Hallmark card exhibit. In May 1984, the first anniversary of Sculley's arrival arrived, and Jobs invited him to a dinner party at Le Mouton Noir, an excellent restaurant in the hills southwest of Cupertino. To Sculley's amazement, Jobs had assembled the Apple board of directors, senior executives, and even some East Coast investors. In response, Sculley waxed poetic on the pleasures of being Jobs' partner for the past year, concluding with a line that, for various reasons, everyone at the table found memorable. "Apple has one leader," he explained, "Steve Jobs and me." He looked across the room, caught Jobs' eye, and smiled. With Lisa sales almost non-existent and Macintosh sales plummeting below ten thousand per month at the end of 1984, Jobs took a terrible, and unusual, decision out of desperation. He decided to take the stock of unsold Lisas, graft on a Macintosh-emulation application, and resell them as the "Macintosh XL." It was a unique instance of Jobs developing something he did not believe in because the Lisa had been discontinued and would not be revived. "I was furious because the Mac XL wasn't real," Hoffman explained. "It was just to get rid of the extra Lisas." It sold nicely, but we had to stop the dreadful farce, so I resigned."

Burrell Smith was also ready to leave by early 1985. He was concerned that if Jobs attempted to talk him out of it, it would be difficult to quit; the reality distortion field was typically too strong for him to resist. So he devised a plan with Hertzfeld to break away. "I've got it!" he said one day to Hertzfeld. "I know the ideal way to quit that will eliminate the reality distortion field." I'll simply walk into Steve's office, undress, and urinate on his desk. What could he possibly say in response? It is certain to work." Even the brave Burrell Smith, according to the Mac crew, would not have the courage to do so. When he finally decided he needed to take a break, he scheduled a meeting with Jobs around the time of Jobs' birthday party. When he stepped in, he was surprised to see Jobs beaming broadly. "Are you going to do it?" "Are you sure you're going to do it?" Jobs inquired. He was aware of the plan. Smith fixed his gaze on him. "Do I really have to? If I have to, I'll do it." Smith decided against it when Jobs gave him a look. As a result, he resigned quietly and on good terms.

Bruce Horn, another of the great Macintosh engineers, rapidly followed him. When Horn went in to say his final goodbyes, Jobs told him, "Everything that's wrong with the Mac is your fault."

"Well, actually, Steve, a lot of the things that are right with the Mac are my fault, and I had to fight like hell to get those things in," Horn responded.

"You're right," Jobs confessed. "I'll give you 15,000 shares if you agree to stay." When Horn declined the offer, Jobs revealed a softer side. "Well, then, give me a hug," he said. As a result, they hugged. The biggest news that month, though, was Steve Wozniak's resignation from Apple for the second time. Wozniak was working quietly as a mid level engineer in the Apple II division at the time, serving as a humble mascot of the company's roots and remaining as far away from management and corporate politics as he could. He had reason to believe that Jobs did not appreciate the Apple II, which remained the company's cash cow and accounted for 70% of sales at Christmas 1984. "People in the Apple II group were being treated as very unimportant by the rest of the company," he subsequently said. "This was despite the fact that the Apple II had been and would continue to be our company's best-selling product for years." He even forced himself to do something out of character: he called Sculley and chastised him for lavishing so much attention on Jobs and the Macintosh division. Frustrated, Wozniak resolved to quit quietly to start a new firm that would manufacture his invented universal remote control gadget. It would use a simple set of buttons that you could quickly configure to control your television, stereo, and other electronic gadgets. He informed the Apple II division's chief of engineering, but he didn't consider himself significant enough to go outside the channels and inform Jobs or Markkula. Jobs first learned about it when it was reported in the Wall Street Journal. Wozniak had honestly answered the reporter's questions when he called in a sincere manner. Yes, he responded, he felt Apple had been neglecting the Apple II division. "Apple's direction has been horrendously wrong for the past five years," he remarked.

Wozniak and Jobs travelled to the White House together less than two weeks later, where Ronald Reagan honoured them with the inaugural National Medal of Technology. When initially shown a telephone, President Rutherford Hayes stated, "An amazing invention, but who would ever want to use one?"—and then remarked, "I thought at the time that he might be mistaken." Apple did not organise a celebratory dinner because of the unpleasant situation surrounding Wozniak's leaving. Jobs and Wozniak then went for a walk and ate at a sandwich restaurant. They talked amiably, Wozniak recalled, and avoided discussing their differences.

In the spring of 1985, there were numerous causes for the schism between Jobs and Sculley. Some were simply commercial differences, such as Sculley's attempt to maximise profits by keeping the Macintosh price high when Jobs wanted to lower it. The board became more concerned about the upheaval, and in early 1985, Arthur Rock and a group of other angry directors delivered a severe lecture to both. They informed Sculley that he was expected to lead the corporation, and that he should do so with more authority and less zeal to be friends with Jobs. They informed Jobs that his duty was to address the mess at the Macintosh division, not to teach other divisions how to do their jobs. Jobs then went back to his office and typed on his Macintosh, "I will not criticise the rest of the organisation, I will not criticise the rest of the organisation..."

As the Macintosh continued to underperform—sales in March 1985 were just 10% of the budgeted amount—Jobs retreated to his office or walked the corridors berating everyone else for the problems. His mood swings worsened, as did his verbal abuse of people around him. Middle-level executives began to revolt against him. Sculley finally built up the courage to tell Jobs that he should step down as CEO of the Macintosh business at the end of that month. He went to Jobs' office one evening and brought the human resources manager, Jay Elliot, to formalise the encounter. "There is no one who admires your brilliance and vision more than I do," Sculley said to begin. He'd uttered such compliments before, but this time it was evident that a harsh "but" would punctuate the thinking. Yes, there was. "But this is really not going to work," he asserted. The flatteries were interspersed with "buts." "We've developed a great friendship," he remarked, "but I've lost faith in your ability to run the Macintosh division." He also chastised Jobs for calling him a bozo behind his back. Jobs was surprised and responded with an unexpected challenge, suggesting that Sculley assist and coach him more: "You've got to spend more time with me." Then he retaliated. He admitted to Sculley that he knew nothing about computers, was doing a poor job leading the company, and had disappointed Jobs since joining Apple. Then he started crying. Sculley sat there, his fingernails biting.

"I'm going to bring this up with the board," Sculley announced. "I'm going to recommend that you resign from your position as president of the Macintosh division." That is something I want you to know." Jobs was persuaded not to protest and instead to accept work on inventing new technology and goods.

Jobs stepped out of his seat and locked his gaze on Sculley. "I don't believe you're going to do that," he stated. "If you do that, you're going to destroy the company."

Sculley publicly disclosed at the April 11 board meeting that he wished to urge Jobs to stand down as leader of the Macintosh business and instead focus on new product development. The board's most crusty and independent member, Arthur Rock, then spoke. He was fired up with both of them: Sculley for not having the courage to take command in the previous year, and Jobs for "acting like a petulant brat." The board needed to put this disagreement behind them, and in order to do so, it needed to meet personally with each of them. Sculley exited the room to allow Jobs to speak first. Jobs maintained that Sculley was the issue since he was unfamiliar with computers. Jobs was chastised by Rock. He responded, angrily, that Jobs had been acting badly for a year and had no right to be in charge of a division. Even Jobs' staunchest admirer, Phil Schlein, attempted to persuade him to gracefully step down to oversee the company's research department. When it was Sculley's turn to meet privately with the board, he issued an ultimatum: "You can back me, and then I take responsibility for running the company, or we can do nothing, and you're going to have to find yourselves a new CEO." If given the authority, he indicated he would not take the job immediately, but rather ease Jobs into it over the next three months. Sculley received unanimous support from the board. He was granted the authority to fire Jobs anytime he deemed it was appropriate. Jobs recognized Del Yocam, a longstanding colleague, and hugged him as he waited outside the boardroom, knowing full well that he was losing.

Sculley attempted to be conciliatory after the board's decision. Jobs requested that the changeover take place gradually over the following few months, and Sculley agreed. Nanette Buckhout, Sculley's executive assistant, called Jobs later that evening to check how he was doing. He was still in his office, stunned. Sculley had already left when Jobs approached her. He began fluctuating wildly in his emotions toward Sculley once more. "Why did John do this to me?" he wondered. "He had betrayed me." Then he swung in the opposite direction. He suggested that he take some time off to work on repairing his relationship with Sculley. "John's friendship is more important than anything else, and I'm thinking that maybe that's what I should do, concentrate on our friendship."

CHAPTER 10

NeXT

When Jobs returned from Europe in August 1985, he called Stanford biologist Paul Berg to discuss the discoveries being made in gene splicing and recombinant DNA. Berg outlined the challenges of doing experiments in a biology lab, where it could take weeks to develop an experiment and obtain a response. "Why don't you try to simulate them on a computer?" Jobs inquired. Berg responded that such machines were too expensive for academic labs. "Suddenly, he was excited about the possibilities," Berg said. "He had planned to start a new business." He was young and wealthy, and he needed to fill the rest of his time."

Jobs has already canvassed academics to determine their workstation requirements. It was something he had wanted to achieve since 1983, when he went to Brown to show off his Macintosh, only to be informed that it would need a considerably more powerful machine to do anything useful in a university lab. Academic scholars wished for a workstation that was both powerful and intimate. Jobs, as head of the Macintosh division, had initiated a project to create such a machine, nicknamed the Big Mac. It would run a UNIX operating system but with a familiar Macintosh user interface. However, once Jobs was fired from the Macintosh division, his replacement, Jean-Louis Gassée, discontinued the Big Mac. Despite the fact that Jobs was still nominally the chairman of the board, he has not attended any meetings since losing authority. He called Sculley to confirm his attendance and requested that a "chairman's report" item be added to the end of the agenda. He didn't mention what it was about, but Sculley believed it was about the latest reorganisation. Instead, when it was his turn to speak, Jobs told the board about his ambitions to launch a new company. "I've been thinking a lot, and I think it's time for me to get on with my life," he said. "It's obvious that I need to take action." "My age is thirty." He then used some prepared notes to discuss his intention to build a computer for the higher education sector. He assured that the new business would not be competitive with Apple, and that he would only bring a few non-key employees with him. He offered to resign as Apple's chairman, but he expressed hope that they could collaborate. He speculated that Apple would seek to buy the distribution rights to his product or licence Macintosh software to it. Mike Markkula was irritated by the prospect of Jobs hiring anyone from Apple. "Why would you take anyone at all?" he questioned. "Don't get upset," Jobs told him and the rest of the board. "These are low-level employees you won't miss, and they're leaving anyway." The board originally appeared to wish Jobs luck in his initiative. After a secret meeting, the board of directors even offered that Apple take a 10% investment in the new firm and keep Jobs on the board. That night, Jobs and his five renegades had dinner at his residence. He was in favour of making the Apple investment, but the others persuaded him that it was a bad idea. They also agreed that it would be better if they resigned immediately. They might then make a clean break. So Jobs wrote a formal letter informing Sculley of the five departures, signed it in his spidery lowercase signature, and travelled to Apple the next morning to present it to him before his 7:30 staff meeting.

"Steve, these are not low-level people," Sculley pointed out. "Well, these people were going to resign anyway," Jobs countered. "They're going to hand in their resignations by nine o'clock this morning."

By 1985, families were beginning to purchase home computers. College students frequently used computers to complete assignments. Steve Jobs was not done with the computer industry. He wanted to prove to Apple that they were incorrect about him. He established a new business. He named it NeXT because it was the next stage in computer technology. He planned to sell his new computers to universities all around the country. They would collaborate with students and lecturers.

However, Steve's concept for the perfect computer was costly. He commissioned a well-known designer to create a logo for his new company. One hundred thousand dollars was spent on the logo! In three years, NeXT lost ten million dollars. Steve invested more and more of his personal money in the business. But no one was buying his machines. They were too pricey. Colleges couldn't afford computers that cost $6,500 each.

Nothing was going as planned at NeXT. But he persisted. He attempted to run the company differently than Apple. He referred to NeXT personnel as "members" of the "community." He paid people based on how long they had been with NeXT. He frequently gave raises. Steve might be generous, but he remained the same demanding boss that he had always been.

CHAPTER 11

PIXAR

When Jobs was struggling at Apple in the summer of 1985, he went for a stroll with Alan Kay, who had previously worked at Xerox PARC and was now an Apple Fellow. Kay knew Jobs was interested in the junction of creativity and technology, so he suggested they meet with a friend of his, Ed Catmull, who was directing the computer branch of George Lucas' film studio at the time. They hired a limo and drove up to Marin County, near Lucas' Skywalker Ranch, where Catmull and his small computer section were based. "I was blown away, and I came back and tried to convince Sculley to buy it for Apple," Jobs said. "But the people in charge at Apple were uninterested, and they were too busy kicking me out anyway." The Lucasfilm computer division created gear and software for producing digital graphics, as well as a team of computer animators that created short films under the direction of a creative cartoon-loving executive named John Lasseter. Lucas, who had completed his first Star Wars trilogy, was going through a divorce and needed to sell the division. He advised Catmull that he needed to find a buyer as quickly as possible. After a few possible buyers declined in the fall of 1985, Catmull and his colleague Alvy Ray Smith decided to seek investors to buy the division themselves. So they dialled Jobs' number, scheduled another meeting, and drove down to his Woodside home. After ranting for a time about Sculley's foibles and foibles, Jobs proposed that he buy their Lucasfilm division altogether. Catmull and Smith objected, saying they wanted an investor rather than a new owner. But Apple soon became evident that there was a happy medium: Jobs could buy a majority stake in the business and serve as chairman while Catmull and Smith ran it.

"I really wanted to buy it because I was really into computer graphics," Jobs said. "I realised they were far ahead of others in combining art and technology, which is what I've always been interested in." He proposed paying Lucas $5 million in addition to investing another $5 million to capitalise the division as a separate company. That was significantly less than Lucas had asked for, but the timing was perfect. They decided to strike a deal. Jobs was considered arrogant and prickly by Lucasfilm's chief financial officer, so when it came time to conduct a meeting with all the stakeholders, he told Catmull, "We have to establish the right pecking order." The plan was for everyone to gather in a room with Jobs, and then the CFO would arrive a few minutes late to prove that he was in charge of the meeting. "But then something funny happened," Catmull recounted. "Steve started the meeting on time without the CFO, and by the time the CFO walked in, Steve was already in control of the meeting."

Jobs only met with George Lucas once, who cautioned him that the people in the division were more interested in making animated movies than in making computers. "You know, these guys are hell-bent on animation," Lucas remarked. "I did warn him that was basically Ed and John's agenda," Lucas subsequently recalled. "I believe he bought the company in his heart because that was also his agenda."

In January 1986, the final agreement was reached. It stated that in exchange for his $10 million investment, Jobs would own 70% of the company, with the remaining stock going to Ed Catmull, Alvy Ray Smith, and the thirty-eight other original workers, down to the receptionist. The Pixar Image Computer was the division's most essential piece of hardware, and it was named for it.

CHAPTER 12

THE RELATIONSHIP IS PAST

Jobs met Joan Baez in 1982, while still working on the Macintosh, through her sister Mimi Faria, who managed a charity that was trying to acquire donations of computers for prisons, and Mark Vermilion, who led Baez's human rights group Humanitas. When Jobs gave them some computers, he asked to meet with Baez. He and Baez had lunch in Cupertino a few weeks later. "I wasn't expecting a lot, but she was really smart and funny," he recalls. He was reaching the end of his romance with Barbara Jasinski at the time. They'd spent time together in Hawaii, shared a house in the Santa Cruz highlands, and even attended one of Baez's concerts. As his relationship with Jasinski deteriorated, Jobs became increasingly serious with Baez. He was twenty-seven and Baez was forty-one, but they had a romance for a few years. "It turned into a serious relationship between two accidental friends who became lovers," Jobs reflected wistfully. Elizabeth Holmes, a Reed College classmate of Jobs's, claimed that one of the reasons he went out with Baez, aside from the fact that she was gorgeous, humorous, and talented, was that she had once been Bob Dylan's lover. "Steve loved that connection to Dylan," she explained later. After being lovers in the early 1960s, Baez and Dylan toured as friends, including with the Rolling Thunder Revue in 1975. (Jobs has bootlegs of those shows.)

Baez had a fourteen-year-old son, Gabriel, from her marriage to anti war campaigner David Harris when she met Jobs. She told Jobs at lunch that she was attempting to teach Gabe how to type. "You mean like on a typewriter?" Jobs inquired. When she responded yes, he countered, "But a typewriter is antiquated."

"If a typewriter is antiquated, what does that make me?" she wondered. There was a strange pause. "As soon as I said it, I realised the answer was so obvious," Baez later told me. The question hung in the balance. "I was horrified."

To the surprise of the Macintosh team, Jobs stormed into the office one day with Baez and showed her the Macintosh prototype. Given his fixation with secrecy, they were astounded that he would show the computer to an outsider, but they were even more astounded to be in the presence of Joan Baez. He handed Gabe an Apple II and eventually a Macintosh to Baez. During his visits, Jobs would point out the elements he appreciated. "He was sweet and patient, but his knowledge was so advanced that he had trouble teaching me," she recounted. He had become a multimillionaire overnight; she was a world-famous star, but she was wonderfully down-to-earth and not particularly wealthy. She didn't know what to make of him at the time, and she still finds him perplexing almost thirty years later. Jobs mentioned Joan Baez and his Polo Shop over a meal early in their relationship, which she claimed she had never visited. "There's a beautiful red dress there that would be perfect for you," he added, driving her to the Stanford Mall boutique. "I said to myself, far out, terrific, I'm with one of the world's richest men and he wants me to have this beautiful dress," Baez remembered. When they arrived at the store, Jobs purchased a few shirts for himself and showed her the red dress. "You ought to buy it," he said. She was taken aback and told him she couldn't really afford it. He said nothing, and they walked away. "Wouldn't you think that if someone talked like that the whole evening, they'd get it for you?" she remarked, clearly perplexed by the occurrence. "You hold the key to unlocking the mystery of the red gown." "I felt strange about it." He would give her laptops but not dresses, and when he gave her flowers, he would explain that they were left over from an office event. "He was both romantic and afraid to be romantic," she described him.

He went to Baez's house in Woodside while working on the NeXT computer to demonstrate to her how beautifully it could generate music. "He had it play a Brahms quartet, and he told me that eventually computers would sound better than humans playing it, even getting the innuendo and cadences better," Baez said. The thought revolted her. "He was working himself up into a fervour of delight, while I was shrinking into a rage and thinking, How could you defile music like that?"

Jobs would tell Debi Coleman and Joanna Hoffman about his relationship with Baez and express concern about marrying someone who had a teenage kid and was presumably past the point of having further children. "At times, he would dismiss her as an 'issues' singer rather than a true 'political' singer like Dylan," Hoffman added. "She was a strong woman, and he wanted to demonstrate his dominance." Plus, he always maintained he wanted to have a family, and he realised he couldn't be with her."

So, after around three years, they dissolved their romance and became just friends. "I thought I was in love with her, but I just really liked her a lot," he later admitted. "We were not meant to be together. I wanted children, but she did not." Baez stated on her divorce from her spouse and why she never remarried in her 1989 memoir: "I belonged alone, which is how I have been since then, with occasional interruptions that are mostly picnics." At the end of the book, she thanks "Steve Jobs for forcing me to use a word processor by putting one in my kitchen."

CHAPTER 13

LOCATING JOANNE AND MONA

A year after Jobs was fired from Apple, his mother Clara, a smoker, was diagnosed with lung cancer when he was thirty-one. He spent time at her deathbed, talking to her in ways he had rarely done before and asking topics he had previously avoided. "When you and Dad got married, were you a virgin?" he inquired. It was difficult for her to speak, but she faked a grin. That's when she revealed she'd previously been married to a man who never returned from the war. She also went into more detail about how she and Paul Jobs came to adopt him.

Soon later, Jobs was able to find out the woman who had placed him for adoption. His silent search for her had begun in the early 1980s, when he engaged a detective who had failed to produce any results. Then Jobs discovered a San Francisco doctor's name on his birth certificate. "He was in the phone book, so I gave him a call," Jobs remembered. The doctor was of no assistance. He stated that a fire had destroyed his records. That was not the case. In reality, shortly after Jobs' phone call, the doctor drafted a letter, sealed it in an envelope, and addressed it to "To be delivered to Steve Jobs on my death." When he died not long after, his wife forwarded the letter to Jobs. In it, the doctor informed that his mother was Joanne Schieble, an unmarried graduate student from Wisconsin.

It took a few more weeks and the efforts of another detective to find her. Joanne had married his biological father, Abdulfattah "John" Jandali, after giving him up, and they had another child, Mona. Jandali left them five years later, and Joanne married George Simpson, a flamboyant ice-skating instructor. That marriage also didn't last long, and in 1970 she embarked on a meandering path that led her and Mona (both of whom now go by the surname Simpson) to Los Angeles.

Jobs was hesitant to tell Paul and Clara, whom he considered his biological parents, about his search for his birth mother. He feared that his parents might be offended, which was rare for him and demonstrated his strong care for them. As a result, he did not contact Joanne Simpson until after Clara Jobs died in early 1986. "I never wanted them to feel like I didn't consider them my parents because they were totally my parents," he said. "I loved them so much that I never wanted them to know about my search, and I even had reporters keep it quiet when any of them found out." When Clara died, he decided to tell Paul Jobs, who was fine with it and indicated he didn't object if Steve contacted his biological mother.

So one day, Jobs called Joanne Simpson, introduced himself, and agreed to see her in Los Angeles. Later, he stated it was mostly out of curiosity. "I believe that environment, rather than heredity, determines your traits," he says, "but you have to wonder a little about your biological roots." He also wanted to reassure Joanne that all she had done was fine. "I wanted to meet my biological mother primarily to check on her well-being and to thank her for saving my life." She was twenty-three years old and had gone through a lot to have me."

When Jobs arrived at Joanne's Los Angeles home, she was filled with emotion. She knew he was renowned and wealthy, but she wasn't sure why. She instantly began to express her feelings. She had been pressed to sign the documents giving him up for adoption, she claimed, and had only done so after being assured that he was content in the home of his adoptive parents. She had always missed him and felt guilty for what she had done. She apologised repeatedly, even as Jobs assured her that he understood and that everything was OK.

She told Jobs, when she had cooled down, that he had a full sister, Mona Simpson, who was then an aspiring author in Manhattan. She'd never informed Mona she had a brother, and she broke the news, or at least part of it, over the phone that day. "You have a brother, and he's wonderful, and he's famous, and I'm going to bring him to New York so you can meet him," she explained. Mona was in the midst of finishing Anywhere but Here, a novel about her mother and their journey from Wisconsin to Los Angeles. Those who have read it will not be shocked that Joanne was slightly eccentric in her delivery of the news about her brother to Mona. She refused to reveal his identity, only that he had been poor, became wealthy, was good-looking and famous, had long dark hair, and lived in California. Mona then worked at George Plimpton's literary publication, the Paris Review, which was headquartered on the first floor of his mansion near Manhattan's East River. Her coworkers and she started a guessing game about who her brother was. What about John Travolta? That was one of the most popular guesses. Other actors were also considered. Someone did speculate at one point that "maybe it's one of those guys who started the Apple computer," but no one could recollect their names.

The meeting occurred in the lobby of the St. Regis Hotel. "He was totally straightforward and lovely, just a normal and sweet guy," Mona recalled. They all sat and talked for a few minutes, then he took his sister for a long walk, just the two of them. Jobs was thrilled to find that he had a sibling who was so similar to him. They were both intense in their artistry, observant of their surroundings, and sensitive yet strong-willed. When they went to dinner together, they noticed the same architectural details and talked about them excitedly afterward. "My sister's a writer!" he exalted to colleagues at Apple when he found out.

When Plimpton threw a party for Anywhere but Here in late 1986, Jobs flew to New York to accompany Mona to it. They grew increasingly close, though their friendship had the complexities that might be expected, considering who they were and how they had come together. "Mona was not completely thrilled at first to have me in her life and have her mother so emotionally affectionate toward me," he later said. "As we got to know each other, we became really good friends, and she is my family. I don't know what I'd do without her. I can't imagine a better sister. My adopted sister, Patty, and I were never close." Mona likewise developed a deep affection for him, and at times could be very protective, although she would later write an edgy novel about him, A Regular Guy, that described his quirks with discomforting accuracy.

One of the few things they would argue about was her clothes. She dressed like a struggling novelist, and he would berate her for not wearing clothes that were "fetching enough." At one point his comments so annoyed her that she wrote him a letter: "I am a young writer, and this is my life, and I'm not trying to be a model anyway." He didn't answer. But shortly after, a box arrived from the store of Issey Miyake, the Japanese fashion designer whose stark and technology-influenced style made him one of Jobs's favourites. "He'd gone shopping for me," she later said, "and he'd picked out great things, exactly my size, in flattering colours." There was one pantsuit that he had particularly liked, and the shipment included three of them, all identical. "I still remember those first suits I sent Mona," he said. "They were linen pants and tops in a pale greyish green that looked beautiful with her reddish hair."

CHAPTER 14

THE LOST FATHER

Meanwhile, Mona Simpson had been searching for their father, who had vanished when she was five years old. She was introduced to a retired New York cop who had founded his own detective business by famed Manhattan authors Ken Auletta and Nick Pileggi. Simpson recounted, "I paid him what little money I had," but the search was unsuccessful. Then she met another private investigator in California, who was able to locate Abdulfattah Jandali's residence in Sacramento through a Department of Motor Vehicles search. Simpson informed her brother and flew from New York to see the man who appeared to be their father. Jobs had no desire to meet with him. "He didn't treat me very well," he subsequently said. "I have nothing against him; I'm just glad to be alive." But what concerns me the most is how he treated Mona. He deserted her." Jobs had abandoned his own illegitimate daughter, Lisa, and was now attempting to reestablish their relationship, but this complication did not change his love toward Jandali. Simpson travelled to Sacramento by himself.

"It was very intense," Simpson said. Her father was working in a little restaurant, which she discovered. He seemed pleased to see her, yet weirdly unconcerned with the situation. They talked for a few hours, and he told me that once he left Wisconsin, he got out of teaching and into the restaurant industry. Simpson had been asked not to mention Jobs, so she didn't. However, her father casually said that he and her mother had another baby, a male, before she was born. "What happened to him?" She was curious. "We'll never see that baby again," he said. That infant is no longer with us." Simpson backed up but said nothing. An even more startling finding came as Jandali was explaining his prior establishments. He asserted that there had been several great ones, fancier than the Sacramento establishment they were then seated in. He told her, a little tearfully, that he wished she had seen him while he was operating a Mediterranean restaurant north of San Jose. "That was a wonderful place," he remarked. "Every successful technology person used to come there. Steve Jobs, too." Simpson was taken aback. "Oh, yeah, he used to come in, and he was a sweet guy, and he was a big tipper," her father added. Mona was able to keep from exclaiming, "Steve Jobs is your son!"

After the visit, she called Jobs from the restaurant's pay phone and planned to meet him at the Espresso Roma café in Berkeley. He invited Lisa, now in grade school, who lived with her mother, Chrisann, to add to the personal and family turmoil. It was about 10 p.m. when they all gathered in the café, and Simpson told them the story. When she described the eatery in San Jose, Jobs was obviously taken aback. He could remember being there and even meeting his biological father. "It was amazing," he said afterwards of the revelation. "I'd been to that restaurant a few times before, and I recall meeting the owner." He was from Syria. Balding. We exchanged handshakes."

Nonetheless, Jobs had no desire to visit him. "I was a wealthy man by then, and I didn't trust him not to try to blackmail me or go to the press about it," he recounted, rather harshly given his lack of knowledge about Jandali. "I specifically asked Mona not to tell him about me."

She never did, but Jandali saw his relationship with Jobs described online years later. (A blogger discovered Simpson named Jandali as her father in a reference book and deduced that he must also be Jobs' father.) Jandali was married for the fourth time at the time and working as a food and beverage manager at the Boomtown Resort and Casino in Reno, Nevada. When he brought his new wife, Roscille, to see Simpson in 2006, he brought up the subject. "What's this thing about Steve Jobs?" he inquired. She corroborated the account, but added that she believed Jobs had no desire to meet with him. Jandali appeared to accept this. "My father is thoughtful and a beautiful storyteller, but he's very, very passive," Simpson explained. "He's never contacted Steve."

Simpson's hunt for Jandali inspired her second novel, The Lost Father, which was released in 1992. (Jobs persuaded Paul Rand, the designer behind the NeXT logo, to create the cover, but according to Simpson, "it was God-awful and we never used it.") She also hunted out numerous Jandali family relatives in Homs and America, and was working on a novel on her Syrian ancestors in 2011. The Syrian ambassador in Washington hosted a dinner for her, which was attended by a cousin and his wife who lived in Florida at the time and had travelled up for the event. Simpson expected Jobs would ultimately meet Jandali, but as time passed, he became less interested. When Jobs and his son, Reed, attended Simpson's birthday dinner in her Los Angeles home in 2010, Reed spent some time looking at images of his biological grandfather, but Jobs disregarded them. He also didn't seem to care about his Syrian ancestry. Even after Syria was swept up in the 2011 Arab Spring events, the issue of the Middle East did not engage him or elicit his usual passionate opinions. "I don't think anybody really knows what we should be doing over there," he replied when asked if the Obama administration should intervene more in Egypt, Libya, and Syria. "You're fucked if you do it, and fucked if you don't."

Lisa Brennan, on the other hand, did not have a happy childhood. Her father practically never came to see her when she was a child. "I didn't want to be a father, so I wasn't," Jobs later admitted, his voice tinged with regret. Nonetheless, he felt the tug on occasion. When Lisa was three, Jobs was driving near the house he had purchased for her and Chrisann when he decided to pull over. Lisa had no idea who he was. He sat on the front porch, not going inside, and talked to Chrisann. The scene played out once or twice a year. Jobs would drop over unannounced, talk briefly about Lisa's school options or other concerns, and then drive away in his Mercedes. However, by the time Lisa was eight, in 1986, the visits had become more frequent. Jobs was no longer consumed by the arduous effort to develop the Macintosh or the subsequent power conflicts with Sculley. He was at NeXT, which was calmer and nicer, and was based in Palo Alto, close to Chrisann and Lisa's house. Furthermore, by third grade, it was apparent that Lisa was a bright and artistic child who had previously been singled out by her instructors for her writing abilities. She was lively and upbeat, with a little of her father's stubborn demeanour. She resembled him as well, with arched brows and a vaguely Middle Eastern angularity. To the amazement of his coworkers, he brought her to the workplace one day. "Look at me!" she exclaimed as she spun cartwheels along the corridor. Avie Tevanian, a tall and outgoing engineer at NeXT who had become Jobs' friend, recalls that when they were heading out to dinner, they would swing by Chrisann's house to pick up Lisa every now and then. "He was very sweet to her," Tevanian said. "He and Chrisann were both vegetarians, but she wasn't. That was alright with him. He advised her to get chicken, which she did."

Eating chicken became her tiny luxury as she moved between two vegetarian parents who had a spiritual reverence for natural foods. "We bought our groceries—our puntarella, quinoa, celeriac, and carob-covered nuts—in yeasty-smelling stores where the women didn't dye their hair," she later wrote about her mother's time with her. "However, we did occasionally sample foreign delicacies." We bought a hot, seasoned chicken from a gourmet shop with rows and rows of chicken spinning on spits and ate it with our fingers in the car from the foil-lined paper bag." Her father, whose food obsessions came in fits and starts, was more particular about what he ate. She saw him spit down a mouthful of soup after discovering it included butter one day. After a brief reprieve at Apple, he was back to being a strict vegan. Lisa realised at a young age that his nutrition obsessions reflected a life philosophy in which asceticism and minimalism may heighten later sensations. "He believed that great harvests came from arid sources, and pleasure came from restraint," she explained. "He knew the equations that most people didn't know: things led to their polar opposites."

Similarly, her father's absence and coldness made his brief moments of tenderness all the more emotionally satisfying. "I didn't live with him, but he would stop by our house some days, a deity among us for a few tingling moments or hours," she recounted. Lisa eventually piqued his attention enough for him to accompany her on walks. He would also accompany her on rollerblades through the calm neighbourhoods of ancient Palo Alto, frequently stopping at the homes of Joanna Hoffman and Andy Hertzfeld. When he initially took her around to meet Hoffman, he just knocked on the door and said, "This is Lisa." Hoffman recognized it right away. "It was obvious she was his daughter," she explained to me. "No one else has that jaw. It's a trademark jaw." Hoffman, who had grown up without knowing her own divorced father, encouraged Jobs to be a better father. He listened to her advice and afterwards thanked her. He once took Lisa to Tokyo for business, where they stayed at the elegant and businesslike Okura Hotel. Jobs ordered enormous trays of unagi sushi at the exquisite downstairs sushi bar, a dish he loved so much that the warm grilled eel passed inspection as vegetarian. Lisa recalled how the chunks melted in her mouth after being covered with fine salt or a thin sweet sauce. The distance between them grew as well. "It was the first time I'd felt, with him, so relaxed and content, over those trays of meat; the excess, the permission and warmth after the cold salads, meant a previously inaccessible space had opened," she later wrote. Under the enormous ceilings with the little chairs, the steak, and myself, he was less rigid with himself, even human."

However, it was not always sweet and light. Jobs was as erratic with Lisa as he was with practically everyone else, swinging between embrace and rejection. On one visit, he was playful; on the next, he was cold; and on many occasions, he was not present at all. "She was always unsure of their relationship," Hertzfeld says. "I went to her birthday party, and Steve was supposed to come, but he was extremely late." She became quite frightened and disappointed. But when he eventually arrived, she lit up."

Lisa learnt to be volatile in response. Their relationship would be a roller coaster ride throughout the years, with each low point exacerbated by their common stubbornness. They could go months without speaking to one other after a fight. Even when he was dealing with chronic health issues, neither of them was excellent at reaching out, apologising, or making an effort to heal. He was wistfully perusing through a box of old pictures with me one day in the fall of 2010, and hesitated over one that showed him visiting Lisa when she was small. "I probably didn't go over there nearly enough," he admitted. Because he hadn't spoken to her in a year, I inquired if he may contact her via phone or email. He gave me a blank stare before returning to rummaging through other old images.

CHAPTER 15

FAMILY MAN

A matchmaker may have put together a composite sketch of the woman who would be suitable for Jobs based on his dating history by this point. Intelligent but unpretentious. Tough enough to stand up to him, but calm enough to soar above the chaos. Well-educated and self-sufficient, but willing to make concessions for himself and a family. Down-to-earth, but with an otherworldly touch. Smart enough to know how to manage him, but secure enough not to have to. And being a stunning, lanky blonde with an easygoing sense of humour who enjoys organic vegetarian meals wouldn't hurt. After his divorce with Tina Redse in October 1989, just such a woman entered his life. More specifically, such a woman entered his classroom. One Thursday evening, Jobs agreed to give one of the "View from the Top" lectures at Stanford Business School. Laurene Powell, a fresh graduate student at the business school, was persuaded to attend the lecture by a guy in her class. They arrived late and discovered that all of the seats were taken, so they sat in the aisle. Powell took her buddy down to the first row and commandeered two of the designated seats when an usher informed them they had to relocate. When Jobs arrived, he was directed to the one next to her. "I looked to my right, and there was a beautiful girl there, so we started chatting while I was waiting to be introduced," Jobs said. Laurene joked that she was sitting there because she had won a lottery, and the prize was that he would take her to supper. "He was so adorable," she stated later. Jobs lingered on the stage's edge after his speech, interacting with kids. He saw Powell leave, then return and wait at the fringe of the gathering before leaving again. He dashed out after her, brushing past the dean, who was attempting to engage him in conversation. "Excuse me, wasn't there something about a raffle you won, that I'm supposed to take you to dinner?" he questioned after catching up with her in the parking lot. She burst out laughing. "How about this Saturday?" he said. She agreed and took down her phone number. Jobs got into his car and drove up to the Thomas Fogarty vineyard in the Santa Cruz foothills above Woodside, where a dinner was being held for the NeXT education sales group. But then he came to a halt and turned around. "I thought, wow, I'd rather have dinner with her than with the education group, so I ran back to her car and said, 'How about dinner tonight?'" She agreed. It was a gorgeous fall evening, and they walked into Palo Alto to St. Michael's Alley, a quirky vegetarian restaurant where they ended up staying for four hours. "We've been together ever since," he declared.

Avie Tevanian was waiting for the rest of the NeXT education group at the vineyard restaurant. "Steve was occasionally unreliable, but when I talked to him, I realised something special had happened," he explained. Powell called her close friend Kathryn (Kat) Smith, who was at Berkeley, shortly after midnight and left a message on her answering machine. "You will not believe what has just happened to me!" it exclaimed. "You will not believe whom I met!" Smith returned the call the next morning and heard the story. "We were aware of Steve, and he was a person of interest to us because we were business students," she explained. Powell later stated that she was not looking forward to meeting Jobs and that the meeting was purely coincidental. She only went because her friend asked her to, and she was a little puzzled about who they were going to visit. "I knew Steve Jobs was the speaker, but the face that came to mind was Bill Gates," she recalled. "I jumbled them up. It was 1989. He was working at NeXT, and he didn't mean much to me. I wasn't very excited, but my friend was, so we went."

"There were only two women in my life that I was truly in love with, Tina and Laurene," Jobs later admitted. "I thought I was in love with Joan Baez, but she was really just someone I liked a lot." Tina and Laurene were the only ones."

Laurene Powell was born in 1963 in New Jersey and learnt to be self-sufficient at a young age. Her father was a Marine Corps pilot who died a hero in a crash in Santa Ana, California; he was leading a crippled plane in for a landing when it collided with his plane, and instead of ejecting in time to save his life, he kept flying in a failed attempt to avoid a residential area. Her mother's second marriage was a terrible situation, but she couldn't leave because she couldn't maintain her enormous family. Laurene and her three brothers had to suffer in a tight household for 10 years, maintaining a nice exterior while compartmentalising troubles. She performed admirably. "The lesson I learned was clear, that I always wanted to be self-sufficient," she explained. "I was proud of that. My connection with money is that it is a tool to help me be self-sufficient, but it is not a part of who I am."

She worked at Goldman Sachs as a fixed income trading strategy after graduating from the University of Pennsylvania, working with large sums of money that she traded for the house account. Her supervisor, Jon Corzine, tried to persuade her to continue at Goldman, but she concluded the work was unsatisfying. "You could be really successful," she continued, "but you're just contributing to capital formation." So she departed after three years and moved to Florence, Italy, where she lived for eight months until enrolling at Stanford Business School. She invited Jobs to her Palo Alto residence on Saturday after their Thursday night meal. Kat Smith drove down from Berkeley pretending to be her roommate in order to meet him. Their relationship grew very heated. "They would kiss and make out," Smith remarked. "He was smitten by her. He'd call me up and ask, 'What do you think, does she like me?' Here I am in this strange situation of having this famous person phone me."

On New Year's Eve 1989, the three travelled to Chez Panisse, the legendary Alice Waters restaurant in Berkeley, with Lisa, who was eleven at the time. Something happened at the dinner that sparked an argument between Jobs and Powell. Powell ended up spending the night at Kat Smith's apartment after they parted ways. The next morning, at nine a.m., there was a tap on the door, and Smith opened it to find Jobs standing outside in the drizzle, clutching some wildflowers he had chosen. "May I please come in and see Laurene?" he said. He entered the bedroom while she was still sleeping. Smith sat in the living room for several hours, unwilling to go in and fetch her clothes. She finally threw on a coat over her nightgown and went to Peet's Coffee to get some breakfast. Jobs didn't appear until after noon. "Kat, can you come here for a minute?" he inquired. They all congregated in the bedroom. "As you know, Laurene's father passed away, and Laurene's mother isn't here, so since you're her best friend, I'm going to ask you the question," he explained. "I want to marry Laurene." Will you grant your approval?"

Smith climbed onto the bed and considered it. "Is this okay with you?" Powell inquired. When she nodded, Smith said, "Well, there's your answer."

It was, however, not a conclusive solution. Jobs has a habit of intensely focusing on something and then quickly shifting his eyes away. He would focus on what he wanted, when he wanted, and be unresponsive to other concerns, no matter how hard people tried to encourage him to interact. He was the same manner in his personal life. At times, he and Powell would engage in public displays of affection so passionate that they humiliated everyone around them, including Kat Smith and Powell's mother. He would wake Powell up in the mornings at his Woodside house by blasting "She Drives Me Crazy" by the Fine Young Cannibals on his tape deck. At times, he would completely disregard her. "Steve would fluctuate between intense focus, where she was the centre of the universe, to being coldly distant and focused on work," Smith explained. "He had the ability to focus like a laser beam, and when he did, you basked in the light of his attention." It was quite dark for you as it went to another point of focus. Laurene was completely perplexed."

He didn't raise his marriage proposal again for several months after she accepted it on January 1, 1990. Smith finally addressed him as they were seated on the edge of a Palo Alto sandbox. What was the situation? Jobs responded that he needed to be confident that Powell could handle his lifestyle and personality. She got tired of waiting and moved out in September. He sulked or ignored the situation for a while. Then he realised he was still in love with Tina Redse, so he sent her roses and attempted to persuade her to return to him, maybe even marry him. He wasn't sure what he wanted, so he startled a wide range of friends and acquaintances by asking them for advice. He'd wonder which was more beautiful, Tina or Laurene. Who was their favourite? What woman should he marry? In Mona Simpson's novel A Regular Guy, the Jobs character "asked more than a hundred people who they thought was more beautiful." But that was a work of fiction; in reality, there were probably less than a hundred. After a month of deliberation, he presented her a diamond ring in October 1990, and she returned home. He ultimately made the correct decision. Redse informed friends that if she had returned to Jobs, neither she nor their marriage would have survived. Even though he lamented the spiritual character of his friendship with Redse, he had a considerably more solid relationship with Powell. He liked her, loved her, respected her, and felt at ease with her. He didn't think of her as mystical, but she was a solid anchor in his life. "He is the luckiest guy to have landed with Laurene, who is smart and can intellectually engage him as well as sustain his ups and downs and tempestuous personality," Joanna Hoffman said. "Because she isn't neurotic, Steve might think she's not as mystical as Tina or something." But that's ridiculous." Andy Hertzfeld concurred.

"Laurene resembles Tina, but she is completely different because she is tougher and armour-plated." That is why the marriage is successful." Jobs recognized this as well. Despite his emotional turpitude and occasional meanness, the marriage would prove to be long-lasting, characterised by commitment and faithfulness, surviving the ups and downs and jangling emotional complexities it encountered. Jobs accompanied Powell to his favourite vacation destination in Hawaii, Kona Village, in December. He had started travelling there nine years before, when he had requested his assistant to find a spot for him to escape from Apple. He didn't like the cluster of austere thatched-roof bungalows tucked on a beach on Hawaii's main island at first. It was a family vacation with shared dining. But within hours, he had come to regard it as heaven. He was moved by the simplicity and spare beauty, and he returned whenever he could. He especially enjoyed being there with Powell that December. Their love had grown stronger. He expressed, even more explicitly, his desire to marry her the night before Christmas. Another issue would soon drive that decision. Powell became pregnant while in Hawaii. "We know exactly where it happened," Jobs subsequently jokes. Avie Tevanian determined that Jobs deserved a bachelor's party. This was not as simple as it seems. Jobs did not enjoy partying and did not have a group of male friends. He even didn't have a best man. So the gathering consisted of Tevanian and Richard Crandall, a computer science professor at Reed who had taken a leave of absence to work at NeXT. Tevanian booked a limo, and when they arrived at Jobs' house, Powell opened the door wearing a suit and a false moustache, stating she wanted to come as one of the guys. It was all a joke, but the three guys, none of whom drank, were shortly on their way to San Francisco to see if they could pull off their own pale version of a bachelor party. Tevanian had been unable to obtain reservations at Greens, Jobs' favourite vegetarian restaurant in Fort Mason, so he booked a very posh restaurant at a hotel. "I don't want to eat here," Jobs declared as soon as the bread was brought to the table. He ordered them get up and go, much to Tevanian's chagrin, as he was not yet accustomed to Jobs' restaurant manners. He directed them to Café Jacqueline in North Beach, his favourite soufflé spot, which was undoubtedly a superior pick. Following that, they rode the limo across the Golden Gate Bridge to a bar in Sausalito, where they all ordered shots of tequila but merely sipped them. "It wasn't the best bachelor party ever, but it was the best we could come up with for someone like Steve, and nobody else volunteered," Tevanian recalled. Jobs was grateful. He determined that Tevanian should marry his sister Mona Simpson. Despite the fact that nothing came of it, the thought was a show of affection. Powell was well aware of what she was getting herself into. While she was organising the wedding, the person who would do the calligraphy for the invitations stopped by to show them some alternatives. Because there was no furniture available, she sat on the floor and spread out the samples. Jobs looked around for a few moments before getting up and leaving the room. They waited for him to return, but he never did. Powell eventually went to find him in his room. "Get rid of her," he instructed. "I can't look at her things." It's a shambles."

Steven Paul Jobs, 36, married Laurene Powell, 27, on March 18, 1991, at the Ahwahnee Lodge in Yosemite National Park. The Ahwahnee, which was built in the 1920s, is a gigantic pile of stone, concrete, and timber fashioned in a style that combines Art Deco, the Arts and Crafts movement, and the Park Service's fondness of massive fireplaces. The views are its finest feature. It features floor-to-ceiling windows with views of Half Dome and Yosemite Falls. Approximately fifty people attended, including Steve's father, Paul Jobs, and sister, Mona Simpson. She was accompanied by her fiancé, Richard Appel, a lawyer who later became a television comedy writer. (As a Simpsons writer, he named Homer's mother after his wife.) Jobs insisted on everyone arriving by rented bus; he wanted complete control over the event. The ceremony took place in the solarium, with snow falling heavily and Glacier Point visible in the distance. It was led by Kobun Chino, Jobs' longstanding Soto Zen teacher, who shook a stick, banged a gong, lighted incense, and chanted in a muttering style that most attendees found incomprehensible. "I thought he was drunk," Tevanian added. He didn't. The wedding cake was shaped like Half Dome, the granite pinnacle at the end of Yosemite Valley, but because it was totally vegan—no eggs, milk, or processed products—many of the guests found it inedible. After that, they all went trekking, and Powell's three hulking brothers got into a snowball fight, complete with tackling and roughhousing. "You see, Mona," Jobs told his sister, "Laurene is descended from Joe Namath, and we're descended from John Muir."

Powell shared her husband's passion for natural meals. She had worked part-time at Odwalla, the juice firm, while in business school, where she helped construct the initial marketing plan. She felt it was necessary to have a career after marrying Jobs, having learned as a child the importance of being self-sufficient. So she founded Terravera, a firm that created ready-to-eat organic meals and shipped them to retailers around Northern California. Instead of living in the lonely and somewhat eerie unfurnished Woodside estate, the couple relocated to a nice and inexpensive house on a corner in an old Palo Alto family-friendly neighbourhood. It was a privileged neighbourhood—neighbours included visionary venture capitalist John Doerr, Google's Larry Page, and Facebook's Mark Zuckerberg, as well as Andy Hertzfeld and Joanna Hoffman—but the homes were not ostentatious, and there were no high hedges or long drives shielding them from view. Instead, residences were built on adjacent lots along level, peaceful streets with large sidewalks. "We wanted to live in a neighbourhood where kids could walk to see their friends," Jobs explained later. The house was not designed in the minimalist and modernist style that Jobs would have used if he had started from scratch. It wasn't a large or unique residence that would draw people's attention as they drove down his Palo Alto street. It was developed in the 1930s by Carr Jones, a local designer who specialised in meticulously designed residences in the "storybook style" of English or French country cottages. The two-story red brick building had exposed wood beams and a shingle roof with curving lines; it looked like a rambling Cotswold cottage or a residence where a well-to-do Hobbit might have resided. A mission-style courtyard framed by the house's wings was the only Californian element. The two-story vaulted-ceiling living area was casual, with a tile and terra-cotta floor. At one end, a great triangle window led up to the apex of the ceiling; when Jobs bought it, it had stained glass, as if it were a chapel, but he replaced it with clear glass. He and Powell also expanded the kitchen to incorporate a wood-burning pizza oven and space for a big wooden table, which would become the family's principal gathering spot. The makeover was scheduled to take four months, but it took sixteen months because Jobs continually reworked the design. They also purchased the little house behind them and demolished it to create a backyard, which Powell transformed into a magnificent natural garden full of seasonal flowers, veggies, and herbs. Jobs was captivated by Carr Jones' use of recycled materials, such as used bricks and timber from telephone poles, to create a basic and durable building. The kitchen timbers had been used to produce moulds for the concrete foundations of the Golden Gate Bridge, which was being built at the time the home was erected. "He was a careful craftsman who was self-taught," Jobs explained, pointing out each detail. "He was more concerned with being inventive than with making money, and he never became wealthy." He never left the state of California. His inspiration came from publications in the library and Architectural Digest."

CHAPTER 16

LISA

Lisa's teachers contracted Jobs in the middle of her eighth-grade year. There were major concerns, and she should probably leave her mother's house. So Jobs took Lisa for a walk, inquired about her situation, and offered to let her live with him. She was a mature fourteen-year-old girl who thought about it for two days. She then said yes. She knew exactly which room she wanted: the one next to her father's. When she got there once alone, she tried it out by lying down on the bare floor. Lisa resided with Jobs and Powell for the entire four years of her high school career, and she adopted the name Lisa Brennan-Jobs. He tried to be a decent father, yet he could be cold and aloof at times. Lisa would seek sanctuary with a friendly family that lived nearby when she felt she needed to flee. Powell made an effort to be helpful, and she was the one who attended the majority of Lisa's school events. Lisa appeared to be thriving by the time she was a senior. She became co editor of the school newspaper, The Campanile. She and her classmate Ben Hewlett, grandson of the man who gave her father his first job, discovered secret raises paid to administrators by the school board. She knew she wanted to move east to college when the time came. She applied to Harvard, forging her father's signature because he was out of town, and was accepted for the 1996 class. Lisa interned at Harvard on the college newspaper The Crimson and subsequently the literary journal The Advocate. She took a year abroad at King's College in London after breaking up with her boyfriend. Throughout her undergraduate years, her relationship with her father was difficult. When she returned home, disputes about trivial matters—what was served for dinner, whether she was paying enough attention to her half-siblings—would erupt, and they would not speak for weeks, if not months. The disputes were so heated at times that Jobs stopped backing her. She borrowed money for her Harvard tuition one year from a married couple, both lawyers, who lived down the street in Palo Alto and whose house she occasionally stayed at. Later, Andy Hertzfeld lent Lisa $20,000 when she worried her father would not pay her tuition at Bennington College's graduate writing program. "He was mad at me for making the loan," Hertzfeld said, "but he called early the next morning and had his accountant wire me the money."

There were some pleasant moments over those years, though, such as one summer when Lisa returned home and sang at a benefit concert for the Electronic Frontier Foundation, an advocacy group that promotes access to technology. The concert was held at San Francisco's Fillmore Auditorium, which was made famous by the Grateful Dead, Jefferson Airplane, and Jimi Hendrix. As her father stood in the back cradling his one-year-old daughter, Erin, she sang Tracy Chapman's hymn "Talkin' bout a Revolution" ("Poor people are gonna rise up / And get their share").

Jobs' ups and downs with Lisa persisted even after she relocated to Manhattan as a freelance writer. Jobs' dissatisfaction with Chrisann compounded their troubles. He had purchased a $700,000 house for Chrisann and put it in Lisa's name, but Lisa turned it over to Chrisann, who then sold it and used the proceeds to go with a spiritual advisor and live in Paris. When the money ran out, she moved back to San Francisco and started doing "light paintings" and Buddhist mandalas. "I am a 'Connector' and a visionary contributor to the future of evolving humanity and the ascended Earth," she wrote on her website (which Hertzfeld managed for her). "I experience the forms, colour, and sound frequencies of sacred vibration as I create and live with the paintings." When Chrisann required money for a terrible sinus infection and dental condition, Jobs refused, forcing Lisa to stop speaking to him for a few years. And so the cycle would continue.

Mona Simpson used all of this, as well as her imagination, to create her third novel, A Regular Guy, which was released in 1996. The title character of the book is modelled on Jobs, and it is true to some extent: It exposes Jobs's silent generosity to, and purchase of a special car for, a smart buddy suffering from degenerative bone disease, as well as many ugly aspects of his relationship with Lisa, including his initial denial of paternity. However, other sections are entirely fictitious; for example, Chrisann trained Lisa to drive at a young age, but the book's scenario of "Jane" driving a truck over the mountains alone at the age of five to locate her father never occurred. Furthermore, there are small aspects in the story that, in journalistic jargon, seem too good to be true, such as the character based on Jobs's description in the opening sentence: "He was a man too busy to flush toilets."

The novel's fictitious portrait of Jobs appears harsh on the surface. Simpson's protagonist is unable "to see any need to pander to the wishes or whims of other people." His hygiene is just as suspect as the actual Jobs'. "He didn't believe in deodorant and frequently claimed that if you ate right and used peppermint castile soap, you wouldn't perspire or smell." However, the story is lyrical and nuanced on many levels, and by the conclusion, the reader has a clearer image of a man who loses control of the great firm he established and comes to respect the daughter he abandoned. He dances with his daughter in the closing scene.

Jobs later admitted that he had not read the novel. "I heard it was about me," he explained, "and if it had been about me, I would have gotten really pissed off, and I didn't want to get pissed at my sister, so I didn't read it." However, he told the New York Times a few months after the book's publication that he read it and saw himself in the main character. "About 25% of it is totally me, right down to the mannerisms," he said Steve Lohr, the reporter. "And I'm certainly not telling you which 25%." According to his wife, Jobs glanced at the book and requested her to read it for him to see what he thought of it.

Simpson sent the book to Lisa before it was published, but she only read the first few pages. "In the first few pages, I was confronted with my family, anecdotes, things, thoughts, and myself in the character Jane," she explained. "And sandwiched between the truths was invention—lies to me, made more obvious by their perilous proximity to the truth." Lisa was hurt, and she explained why in a column for the Harvard Advocate. Her first manuscript was somewhat bitter, but she toned it down before publishing it. Simpson's friendship violated her. "I had no idea Mona was collecting for those six years," she wrote. "I had no idea that she, too, was talking as I sought her consolation and advice." Lisa eventually reconciled with Simpson. They went to a coffee shop to talk about the book, and Lisa admitted that she hadn't finished it. Simpson expressed interest in the ending. Lisa had an on-again, off-again relationship with Simpson over the years, but it was closer in some respects than her relationship with her father.

CHAPTER 17

CHILDREN

When Powell gave birth in 1991, a few months after her marriage to Jobs, their infant was known for two weeks as "baby boy Jobs," because deciding on a name was proving to be only marginally easier than deciding on a washing machine. Finally, they gave him the name Reed Paul Jobs. His middle name was that of Jobs' father, and his first name was chosen because it sounded good rather than because it was the name of Jobs' college, according to both Jobs and Powell.

Reed resembled his father in many ways: incisive and intelligent, with intense eyes and a captivating appeal. But, unlike his father, he had good manners and a humble demeanour. He was imaginative—as a child, he liked to dress up and stay in character—and an excellent student who was interested in science. He could imitate his father's glare, but he was clearly friendly and seemed to be devoid of any malice.

Erin Siena Jobs was born in 1995. She grew into a more introspective child with an emotional intelligence that gave her a sensitive understanding of other people's sentiments. She inherited her father's interest in design and architecture, but she also learnt to maintain a certain emotional distance in order not to be hurt by his detachedness.

Eve, the youngest kid, was born in 1998 and grew into a strong-willed, humorous firecracker who knew how to handle her father, argue with him (and occasionally win), and even make fun of him. Her father quipped that if she does not become President of the United States, she will run Apple.

In 1995 Oracle CEO Larry Ellison hosted a fortieth-birthday party for Jobs, which was attended by a slew of industry luminaries and business titans. Ellison had grown close to the Jobs family and would frequently take them out on one of his numerous beautiful yachts. Reed began referring to him as "our rich friend," which was funny proof of his father's aversion to excessive shows of wealth. Jobs learned from his Buddhist days that material possessions frequently cluttered rather than improved life. "Every other CEO I know has a security detail," he pointed out. "They even have them in their homes." It's an insane way to live. We simply determined that was not how we wanted to raise our children."

CHAPTER 18

TOY STORY

The Walt Disney Company had licensed Pixar's Computer Animation Production System, making it the company's largest customer. Lasseter was glued to the screen as he watched the two wiry and tightly wound principals parry and thrust. "Just to see Steve and Jeffrey go at it, I was in awe," he said. "It was like watching a fencing match." They were both lords." But Katzenberg was armed with a sabre, whereas Jobs was just armed with a foil. Pixar was on the verge of bankruptcy and required a deal with Disney significantly more than Pixar required a deal with Disney. Furthermore, Disney could afford to finance the entire venture, whereas Pixar could not. As a result, in May 1991, Disney agreed to buy the film and its characters altogether, retain creative control, and pay Pixar around 12.5% of ticket sales. It had the option (but not the obligation) to do Pixar's next two films, as well as the right to develop sequels to the picture (with or without Pixar). Disney could potentially cancel the picture at any point for a minimal fee. The concept proposed by John Lasseter was dubbed "Toy Story." It arose from his and Jobs' common idea that products had an essence to them, a purpose for which they were created. If the item had feelings, they would be motivated by a desire to fulfil its essence. A glass's purpose is to hold water; if it had feelings, it would be joyful when full and sad when empty. The purpose of a computer screen is to communicate with humans. A bicycle's essence is to be ridden in a circus. Toys' goal is to be played with by children, hence their existential fear is of being discarded or overshadowed by newer toys. So a buddy movie between an old favourite toy and a sparkling new toy would have to include some drama, especially if the action centred around the toys being separated from their child. "Everyone has had the traumatic childhood experience of losing a toy," the original treatment started. Our story is told from the perspective of a toy as he loses and seeks to regain the single most important thing to him: being played with by children. This is the reason for all toys' existence. It is the emotional core of their being."

Toy Story was released in November 1995.

CHAPTER 19

THE SECOND COMING

Apple was able to ride comfortably with a high profit margin for a few years after Jobs was gone due to its temporary dominance in desktop publishing. Back in 1987, while he was feeling like a genius, John Sculley made a series of pronouncements that now sound embarrassing. Sculley wrote that Jobs intended Apple to "become a wonderful consumer products company." "This was a crazy plan...." Apple will never be a consumer goods firm.... We couldn't make our hopes of changing the world come true. High-tech products could not be designed and sold to the general public."

Jobs was outraged, and he grew enraged and disdainful as Sculley presided over Apple's inexorable slide in market share in the early 1990s. "Sculley destroyed Apple by bringing in corrupt people and corrupt values," Jobs complained later. "They were more concerned with making money—primarily for themselves, but also for Apple—than with creating great products." He believed that Sculley's profit-driven approach came at the expense of acquiring market share. "Macintosh lost to Microsoft because Sculley insisted on milking all the profits he could get rather than improving and making the product more affordable." Profits eventually vanished as a result. It took Microsoft a few years to match Macintosh's graphical user interface, but by 1990, the business had released Windows 3.0, launching the corporation's march to desktop domination. When Windows 95 was released in 1995, it quickly became the most successful operating system ever, and Macintosh sales began to decline. "Microsoft simply ripped off what other people did," Jobs subsequently said. "Apple earned it. It didn't create anything fresh after I departed. The Mac didn't fare much better. Microsoft had a sitting duck."

When he gave a talk to a Stanford Business School club at the home of a student, who asked him to autograph a Macintosh keyboard, his irritation with Apple was palpable. Jobs agreed to do so in exchange for the ability to remove the keys that had been introduced to the Mac after he left. He took out his vehicle keys and yanked off the four arrow cursor keys he had previously forbidden, as well as the top row of F1, F2, F3... function keys. "I'm changing the world one keyboard at a time," he said flatly. Then he signed the broken keyboard. Jobs went for a walk down the beach with his friend Larry Ellison, the irrepressible Oracle chairman, during his 1995 Christmas holiday in Kona Village, Hawaii. They contemplated mounting a bid for Apple and reinstalling Jobs as CEO. "I will buy Apple, you will get 25% of it right away for being CEO, and we can restore it to its former glory," Ellison claimed, claiming $3 billion in financing. But Jobs refused. "I decided I'm not a hostile-takeover kind of guy," he said. "It might have been different if they had asked me to return."

Apple's market share had declined to 4% by 1996, from a high of 16% in the late 1980s. Michael Spindler, the German-born CEO of Apple's European operations who took over for Sculley in 1993, attempted to sell the company to Sun, IBM, and Hewlett-Packard. That failed, and he was fired in February 1996 and replaced by Gil Amelio, the CEO of National Semiconductor and a research engineer. During his first year, the firm lost $1 billion, and the stock price, which had been $70 in 1991, fell to $14, despite the fact that other companies were skyrocketing due to the computer boom. Jobs did not appeal to Amelio. Their first meeting was in 1994, shortly after Amelio was elected to the Apple board of directors. Jobs called and said, "I want to come over and see you." Amelio invited him to his office at National Semiconductor, and he later recalled watching Jobs enter through the glass wall of his office. He appeared to be "rather like a boxer, aggressive and elusively graceful, or an elegant jungle cat ready to spring at its prey." After a few minutes of pleasantries—far more than Jobs was accustomed to exchanging—he quickly revealed the reason for his visit. He wanted Amelio to assist him in returning to Apple as CEO. "There's only one person who can rally the Apple troops," Jobs declared, "only one person who can straighten out the company." Jobs believed that the Macintosh age had passed, and it was now time for Apple to produce something equally creative.

"If the Mac dies, what will replace it?" Amelio inquired. Jobs' response did not impress him. "Steve didn't seem to have a clear answer," remarked Amelio later. "He seemed to have a set of one-liners." Amelio was aware of Jobs' reality distortion field and was pleased to be resistant to it. Jobs was escorted out of his office abruptly. Amelio understood he had a significant problem during the summer of 1996. Apple was banking on a new operating system called Copland, but Amelio discovered soon after becoming CEO that it was a bloated piece of vaporware that would not meet Apple's needs for better networking and memory protection, nor would it be ready to ship in 1997 as planned. He openly stated that he will find an alternative as soon as possible. His issue was that he lacked one. So Apple needed a partner capable of developing a robust operating system, particularly one that was UNIX-like and included an object-oriented application layer. There was clearly one business that could provide such software—NeXT—but it would take time for Apple to focus on it. Apple first focused its attention on Be, a firm founded by Jean-Louis Gassée. Gassée began negotiating the sale of Be to Apple, but in August 1996, during a meeting with Amelio in Hawaii, he overplayed his hand. He stated that he wanted to bring his fifty-person team to Apple and requested a 15% stake in the company, valued at approximately $500 million. Amelio was taken aback. He was estimated to be worth around $50 million by Apple. Gassée refused to move from his demand for at least $275 million after several offers and counteroffers. He believed Apple had no alternatives. Gassée told Amelio, "I've got them by the balls, and I'm going to squeeze until it hurts." This did not sit well with Amelio. "Does anyone know Steve well enough to call him out on this?" Amelio enquired of his crew. Amelio didn't want to make the call because his previous interaction with Jobs had gone so horribly. He didn't have to, as it turned out. Apple was already receiving pings from NeXT. Garrett Rice, a mid level product marketer at NeXT, had simply picked up the phone and called Ellen Hancock to ask whether she was interested in looking at its software without consulting Jobs. She dispatched a representative to speak with him. By Thanksgiving

1996, the two businesses had initiated preliminary discussions, and Jobs dialled Amelio directly. "I'm on my way to Japan, but I'll be back in a week, and I'd like to see you as soon as I return," he explained. "Don't make any decisions until we can all get together." Despite his previous interactions with Jobs, Amelio was ecstatic to hear from him and enthralled by the prospect of working with him. "For me, the phone call with Steve was like inhaling the flavours of a great bottle of vintage wine," he said. He promised not to make any deals with Be or anyone else before they were together.

Jobs' competition with Be was both professional and personal. NeXT was in trouble, and the thought of being purchased out by Apple was a tempting lifeline. Furthermore, Jobs kept grudges, sometimes bitterly, and Gassée was towards the top of his list, despite the fact that they had appeared to reconcile while Jobs was at NeXT. "Gassée is one of the few people in my life who I would say is truly horrible," Jobs asserted afterwards, harshly. "He knifed me in the back in 1985." To his credit, Sculley had been kind enough to knife Jobs in the front. Steve Jobs returned to Apple's Cupertino campus for the first time in eleven years on December 2, 1996. He met with Amelio and Hancock in the executive conference room to make the NeXT pitch. He was drawing on the whiteboard again, this time giving his lecture about the four waves of computer systems that, in his opinion, culminated with the advent of NeXT. Despite the fact that he was chatting to two people he didn't respect, he was at his most attractive. He was very skilled at simulating modesty. "It's probably a totally crazy idea," he admitted, but if they liked it, "I'll structure any kind of deal you want—licence the software, sell you the company, whatever." He was eager to sell everything, and he pushed that strategy. "When you look closely, you'll realise you want more than my software," he said. "You'll want to buy the whole company and take all the people."

CHAPTER 20

REVIVAL

Steve was conflicted about returning to Apple. He had negative memories of how he had been treated at Apple. At Pixar, he was already the CEO of a tremendously successful corporation. Erin Sienna, his daughter with Laurene, was born in 1995. Did he truly want to take on a failing business? If it had been any other corporation, the answer would almost certainly have been no. But Apple was his child. He couldn't simply stand by and watch it perish. Steve agreed to serve as Apple's CEO for a limited time. Apple was forced to hunt for a permanent replacement for him. He set himself a yearly compensation of one dollar.

Steve made significant modifications right away. In Boston in 1997, Steve announced to a crowd of Mac fans that Apple would join forces with Microsoft. Were Apple and Microsoft going to collaborate? This was unprecedented! Steve, on the other hand, stated that all Apple computers would use Microsoft's Internet Explorer Web browser. Onstage, there was a massive TV screen behind Steve. The audience booed when Microsoft CEO Bill Gates appeared on the screen. But Steve recognized that the $150 million agreement would benefit Apple. He was correct. The company's worth increased. Other adjustments were done by Steve. He got rid of items that were not selling. He reduced expenses. He fired so many employees that Apple employees were frightened to ride in an elevator with him. They were afraid they wouldn't have a job by the time they got to their floor. Steve continued to insist that he was merely a temporary CEO. "I'm here almost every day, but only for the next few months," he told TIME magazine in 1997. "I'm very clear on it." But he was planning for the future.

Think different

In 1997, in cities across America, a series of posters appeared on buildings, buses, and billboards. The posters showed photos of famous people known for doing something new. There was a poster of Alfred Hitchcock, the famous movie director. Another poster was of Lucille Ball and Desi Arnaz, stars of I Love Lucy. Another poster showed Jim Henson and Kermit the Frog. In the corner of each poster was the Apple logo and two words: THINK DIFFERENT.

The ad campaign was the brainchild of Steve Jobs. He wanted to show what Apple stood for—new ideas, not the "same old, same old." The posters didn't advertise any particular product. But they told the public to be ready because something exciting was happening at Apple. What was happening was the iMac—short for Internet Macintosh. This new personal computer was inexpensive and easy to use. In the 1990s, there was a brand-new pastime—surfing the Web. Steve wanted people to surf on iMacs. He also wanted iMacs to look different. The iMac came in a plastic case in five bright colours inspired by Steve's visit to a jelly bean factory: blueberry, grape, lime, strawberry, and tangerine. Within a year, the iMac became the best-selling computer in the world. That same year, Steve and Laurene had another baby daughter, Eve. Steve's eldest daughter, Lisa, was studying journalism at Harvard University. It was a happy time in Steve's life. Steve had planned to only stay at Apple for a few months. But in 2000, he became the permanent head. He had too many big plans to leave Apple now.

In May 2001, Apple opened its first stores. Just as Apple computers didn't look like other computers, Apple stores were very different, too. Made with a lot of glass, they looked more like works of art. Steve oversaw every step of the design of the stores from the floor tiles to the shelves. Every single detail was important to him.

At the store's Genius Bar, people could ask questions about problems with their machines and get personal training on their computers. Steve had put Apple on top of the personal computer market. As he had predicted, people used their computers for work and also for pleasure. Listening to music was something else people did for fun. In the 1990s, most people listened to music on compact discs (CDs). A CD was like a record album. People bought CDs by their favourite groups and played them on CD players. They were about the size of a butter plate and had better sound than a vinyl record album. But Steve started thinking about something even better. He bought a software program that allowed people to take their favourite songs from a CD and put them on the computer as a digital file. It was called an MP3 file. Once it was on the computer, you didn't need the CD anymore. Steve renamed the program iTunes. Using iTunes, a person could turn their computer into a personal jukebox. Other companies created MP3 players. These were portable machines that hooked up to speakers or headphones and played music files. No CD or cassette tape was needed. Steve Jobs decided that Apple had to make its own player.

In October 2001, at a press event in California, Steve reached into his pocket. He pulled out a thin gadget that was smaller than a bar of Hershey's chocolate. "We call it the iPod," he said. At first, the iPod only worked with Mac computers. But in 2002, Steve agreed to make it work with Microsoft's Windows machines. Now that Windows users could also use the iPod, its sales skyrocketed. Customers loved the iPod.

People in the music industry did not. Most people got the songs they played on their iPods off CDs. The CD didn't have to be theirs. For instance, they could get songs for free from a friend's CD. Songs could also be "shared" over the Internet. Nobody in the music industry could figure out how to make people pay for music that they could get for free illegally. Nobody except Steve. If people could buy music easily and cheaply, he thought they wouldn't mind paying. Because he could "think different," Steve opened the iTunes Music Store in 2003. It was not a regular store; it wasn't in a building. It was a program you downloaded onto a computer. Using his famous powers of persuasion, he made a deal with many record companies to sell their songs on iTunes for ninety-nine cents a piece. On the first day it was open, the iTunes store sold two hundred seventy-five thousand songs. It was so easy to order songs. It didn't cost much. Everyone began buying music over the Internet.

Apple was back on top, and Steve was too. He was still Pixar's CEO. He was also assisting in the upbringing of Reed, Erin, and Eve. Lisa was a Harvard graduate. Laurene, his wife, had started College Track, a charity that assists children from low-income households in getting into college.

CHAPTER 21

CANCER

Jobs would subsequently suggest that his illness was triggered by the arduous year he spent running both Apple and Pixar beginning in 1997. He'd developed kidney stones and other problems from driving back and forth, and he'd arrived home fatigued and unable to speak. "That's probably when this cancer started growing, because my immune system was pretty weak at the time," he explained. There is no evidence that fatigue or a compromised immune system promote cancer. His kidney troubles, however, did indirectly lead to the discovery of his malignancy. He had a chance to run into the urologist who had treated him in October 2003, and she asked him to undergo a CAT scan of his kidneys and ureter. His last scan was five years ago. The fresh scan indicated no problems with his kidneys, but it did show a shadow on his pancreas, so she requested a pancreatic exam. He didn't do it. He was skilled at wilfully disregarding inputs he didn't want to process, as he always was. She persevered, however. "Steve, this is really important," she told him a few days later. "You need to do this." He complied since her tone of voice was urgent. He arrived early one morning, and after reviewing the scan, the physicians met with him to inform him that it was a tumour. One of them even suggested that he get his affairs in order, which was a kind of way of expressing that he might only have a few months to live. That evening, they performed a biopsy by inserting an endoscope down his neck and into his intestines to insert a needle into his pancreas and extract a few tumour cells. Powell recalls her husband's doctors crying with excitement. It was discovered to be an islet cell or pancreatic neuroendocrine tumour, which are rare but slower growing and hence more likely to be effectively treated. He was fortunate that it was discovered so early—as a byproduct of routine renal screening—and hence could be surgically removed before it had spread much. Larry Brilliant, whom he originally met at the ashram in India, was one of his first calls. "Do you still believe in God?" Jobs inquired. Brilliant confirmed this, and they examined the various paths to God given by the Hindu guru Neem Karoli Baba. Then Brilliant inquired of Jobs as to what was wrong. "I have cancer," Jobs said.

Art Levinson, a member of Apple's board of directors, was chairing a board meeting of his own business, Genentech, when his cell phone called and Jobs' name came on the screen. When there was a little pause, Levinson returned his phone and informed him of the malignancy. He was an advisor because he had an expertise in cancer biology and his company developed cancer therapy medications. Andy Grove of Intel, who had battled and defeated prostate cancer, agreed. When Jobs contacted him that Sunday, he immediately drove over to his house and remained for two hours. To the shock of his friends and wife, Jobs refused to have the tumour surgically removed, which was the only acceptable medical method. "I really didn't want them to open up my body, so I tried a few other things to see if a few other things would work," he told me years later, with a sigh of regret. He followed a rigorous vegan diet, drinking copious amounts of fresh carrot and fruit juice. Acupuncture, herbal cures, and other treatments he discovered on the Internet or by interviewing people across the country, including a psychic, were added to his routine. For a time, he was influenced by a herbal therapist who ran a natural health clinic in southern California, emphasising the use of organic herbs, juice fasts, frequent bowel cleansings, hydrotherapy, and the expression of any negative emotions. "The important thing was that he wasn't ready to open his body," Powell recounted. "It's difficult to persuade someone to do something like that." She did, however, make an effort. "The body exists to serve the spirit," she claimed. His buddies advised him to get surgery and chemotherapy. "Steve talked to me when he was trying to cure himself by eating horseshit and horseshit roots, and I told him he was crazy," Grove recounted. Levinson stated that he "pleaded every day" with Jobs and found it "enormously frustrating that I just couldn't connect with him." Their conflicts almost destroyed their friendship. "That's not how cancer works," Levinson maintained when Jobs discussed his diet therapy. "You can't fix this without surgery and a barrage of toxic chemicals." Even Dr. Dean Ornish, a pioneer in alternative and nutritional disease treatment, took a long walk with Jobs and emphasised that traditional treatments were often the best option. "You really need surgery," Ornish said. Jobs' obstinacy lasted nine months after his October 2003 diagnosis. Part of it was caused by the dark side of his reality distortion field. "I think Steve has such a strong desire for the world to be a certain way that he wills it to be that way," Levinson hypothesised. "Sometimes it doesn't work. Reality is harsh." His scary propensity to filter out stuff he didn't want to deal with was the inverse of his marvellous capacity to focus. This contributed to many of his great accomplishments, but it may also backfire. "He has that ability to ignore stuff he doesn't want to confront," Powell added. "That's just how he's wired." Whether it was personal concerns involving his family and marriage, professional issues involving engineering or business challenges, or health and cancer issues, Jobs sometimes simply did not engage. He had previously been rewarded for what his wife referred to as "magical thinking"—his belief that he could compel things to happen as he desired. Cancer, on the other hand, does not work in this manner. Powell enlisted the help of everyone close to him, including his sister Mona Simpson, to try to turn him around. A CAT scan in July 2004 revealed that the tumour had enlarged and may have spread. It forced him to face reality. Jobs had surgery on Saturday, July 31, 2004, at Stanford University Medical Center. He did not have the entire "Whipple procedure," which involves removing a big portion of the stomach and intestine as well as the pancreas. The physicians contemplated it, but settled on a less drastic technique, a modified Whipple that removed only a portion of the pancreas. Jobs announced his procedure to staff the next day through email, using his PowerBook connected to an AirPort Express in his hospital bed. He told them that the sort of pancreatic cancer he had "represents about 1% of the total cases of pancreatic cancer diagnosed each year, and can be cured by surgical removal if diagnosed in time (mine was)." He stated that he would not require chemotherapy or radiation treatment and that he hoped to return to work in September. "While I'm away, I've asked Tim Cook to oversee Apple's day-to-day operations so we don't miss a beat." I'm sure I'll be phoning some of you way too often in August, and I hope to see you in September."

Because of his obsessive diets and strange practices of purging and fasting that he had performed since he was a youngster, one side effect of the operation would become an issue for Jobs. Because the pancreas produces the enzymes that allow the stomach to digest food and absorb nutrients, removing a portion of the organ makes it difficult to obtain adequate protein. Patients are recommended to eat frequently and to follow a nutritious diet that includes a variety of meat and fish proteins, as well as full-fat milk products. Jobs had never done anything like this before, and he never would. He was hospitalised for two weeks and then battled to regain strength. "I remember coming back and sitting in that rocking chair," he explained, indicating one in his living room. "I didn't have the stamina to walk." It took me a week to be able to walk around the block. I forced myself to walk a few blocks to the gardens, then further, and within six months I had virtually all of my energy back." Regrettably, the malignancy had spread. During the procedure, doctors discovered three liver metastases. They would never know if they had operated nine months earlier if they had caught it before it spread. Jobs underwent chemotherapy treatments, which exacerbated his eating difficulties.

CHAPTER 22

EVOLUTION

Steve returned to work. However, he did not appear to be in good health. He was pallid and losing weight. People were concerned that the cancer was spreading again. He didn't say anything about his illness. However, in 2005, he delivered a commencement address to the Stanford University graduating class. Cancer taught him that "time is limited, so don't waste it living someone else's life.... have the courage to follow your heart and intuition."

These were the words that Steve Jobs lived by. He might not have had much time left. So, once again, Steve began to consider how to

Cell phones were ubiquitous by 2005. Steve owned a cell phone, but he disliked it. It neither worked nor looked decent. None of his buddies seemed to like their cell phones. Steve made the decision to create a phone that people would fall in love with. Steve showed the iPhone to the audience at an Apple product launch event in 2007. The iPhone was more than just a phone. It was a powerful personal computer that could be carried in your pocket.

The iPhone rendered all other phones obsolete. Instead of buttons, it used a touch screen. It included e-mail and the Internet. The iPhone could capture images and record video. People couldn't wait to get their hands on an early iPhone, just as they couldn't wait to get their hands on an early Mac. Steve enjoyed being in charge of Apple. However, he began taking time off in early 2009. Steve refused to acknowledge that his cancer had returned. Nonetheless, everyone at Apple was aware of the cause for his absence. Steve also contacted a writer, Walter Isaacson. Isaacson was a biographer. Steve inquired as to whether Isaacson would write his biography. Steve was often reserved. Nonetheless, he was spilling the beans about his personal life. He appeared to be aware that he might not survive much longer. He received a liver transplant in April of that year. Steve, who was half unconscious before his operation, complained that the medical equipment was unsightly and poorly designed! He returned to work a few months later. Despite his illness, he had a new surprise in store for the people. Steve unveiled the iPad, Apple's new tablet computer, in 2010. It was smaller, thinner, and lighter than everything that had come before. Tablet computers had been available for over two decades. But, once again, Steve made it fresh and unique. The iPad was a wireless handheld computer. It was considerably larger than the iPhone, so it was easier to read books, browse the Web, view movies, and play games on it. Apple sold 300,000 iPads in a single day. Apple was on the verge of bankruptcy in 1997. It became the world's most successful firm in August 2011. Steve resigned as CEO the next month. He was no longer physically fit to work. He chose to remain at home with Laurene and their children. Many of Steve's pals, including Bill Gates, came to see him. The two men reminisced about their youth. Steve expressed gratitude to Laurene for keeping him "semi-sane." Bill stated that his wife, Melinda, had done the same thing for him.

By 2005, iPod sales had skyrocketed. That year, an astounding twenty million units were sold, quadrupling the previous year's total. The product was growing more essential to the company's financial line, accounting for 45% of revenue that year, while also burnishing the company's hipness in a way that promoted Mac sales.

That's why Jobs was concerned. "He was always obsessing about what could go wrong," said board member Art Levinson. He had arrived at the following conclusion: "The device that can eat our lunch is the cell phone." As he stated to the board, now that phones have cameras, the digital camera sector is being crushed. The same thing may happen to the iPod if phone manufacturers were to incorporate music players into their devices. "Because everyone has a phone, the iPod may become obsolete."

His first approach was to partner with another company, which he stated in front of Bill Gates was not in his DNA. He began talking to Motorola's new CEO, Ed Zander, about creating a companion to Motorola's popular RAZR, which had a cell phone and digital camera with an iPod built in. As a result, the ROKR was born. It didn't have the appealing minimalism of an iPod or the practical slimness of a RAZR. It was ugly, difficult to load, and had an arbitrary hundred-song limit, all of which indicated that it had been negotiated by a committee, which was contrary to the way Jobs preferred to work. Instead of being controlled by a single business, hardware, software, and content were cobbled together by Motorola, Apple, and the wireless carrier Cingular. "You're calling this the phone of the future?" On its November 2005 cover, Wired scoffed. Jobs was enraged. "I'm sick of dealing with these stupid companies like Motorola," he told Tony Fadell and others at an iPod product review conference. "Let's just do it ourselves." He'd observed something strange about the current crop of cell phones: they all stank, much like portable music players used to. "We would sit around talking about how much we hated our phones," he said. "They were far too complex." They had features that no one could figure out, such as the address book. It was simply Byzantine." George Riley, an Apple outside lawyer, recalls sitting in meetings to discuss legal concerns when Jobs would become bored, grab Riley's phone, and start pointing out all the ways it was "brain-dead." As a result, Jobs and his team were enthusiastic about the potential of creating a phone that they would want to use. "That's the best motivator of all," Jobs stated afterwards. The potential market was another motive. In 2005, over 825 million mobile phones were sold to people ranging from elementary school students to grandmothers. Because the majority were garbage, there was potential for a premium and trendy product, just as there had been in the portable music-player market. On the basis that it was a wireless product, he initially offered the project to the Apple division that was developing the AirPort wireless base station. He soon understood, however, that it was essentially a consumer product, similar to the iPod, and delegated it to Fadell and his teammates. Their first thought was to tweak the iPod. They attempted to use the trackwheel to allow a user to cycle between phone options and enter numbers without using a keyboard. It didn't feel right. "We were having a lot of problems using the wheel, especially getting it to dial phone numbers," Fadell said. "It was cumbersome." It was good for navigating through an address book but terrible for entering data. The team kept attempting to persuade itself that consumers would mostly call people in their contact book, but they realised it wouldn't work.

At that time there was a second project under way at Apple: a secret effort to build a tablet computer. In 2005 these narratives intersected, and the ideas for the tablet flowed into the planning for the phone. In other words, the idea for the iPad actually came before, and helped to shape, the birth of the iPhone. When it came time to introduce the iPhone, Jobs, as usual, decided to give a magazine a unique early peek. He contacted Time Inc.'s editor in chief, John Huey, and began with his usual superlative: "This is the best thing we've ever done." "But there's nobody smart enough at Time to write it," he said, "so I'm going to give it to someone else." Huey referred him to Lev Grossman, a knowledgeable Time magazine technology reporter (and novelist). Grossman accurately emphasised in his post that the iPhone did not invent many new functions, but rather made existing ones more usable. "However, that is significant. When our tools fail, we tend to blame ourselves, blaming ourselves for being too stupid, not reading the manual, or having too-fat fingers. When our tools break, we are broken. And when someone fixes one, we feel a little bit more complete."

Jobs summoned Andy Hertzfeld, Bill Atkinson, Steve Wozniak, and the 1984 Macintosh team for the introduction at Macworld in San Francisco in January 2007, as he had done when he launched the iMac. This may have been his best product presentation in a career full of them. "Every once in a while, a revolutionary product comes along that changes everything," he said to begin. He cited two previous examples: the initial Macintosh, which "changed the whole computer industry," and the first iPod, which "changed the entire music industry." Then he gradually progressed to the product he was about to introduce: "Today, we're introducing three revolutionary products of this class." The first is a touch-controlled widescreen iPod. The second is a game-changing mobile phone. The third is a game-changing Internet communications gadget." "Are you getting it?" he said after repeating the list. This isn't three independent gadgets; it's just one, and we're calling it the iPhone."

Five months later, at the end of June 2007, Jobs and his wife walked to the Apple shop in Palo Alto to take in the enthusiasm. Because he did this frequently on the day new things went on sale, there were some admirers waiting for him, and they greeted him as they would have Moses if he had strolled in to buy the Bible. Hertzfeld and Atkinson were among the devout. "Bill stayed in line all night," Hertzfeld remarked. Jobs began to giggle as he waved his arms. "I sent him one," he explained. Hertzfeld responded, "He needs six."

Bloggers called the iPhone "the Jesus Phone" right away. However, Apple's competitors stressed that success costs too much at $500. "It's the most expensive phone in the world," Microsoft CEO Steve

Ballmer told CNBC. "And it doesn't appeal to business customers because it doesn't have a keyboard." Microsoft had once again undervalued Jobs' product. Apple has sold 90 million iPhones by the end of 2010, accounting for more than half of the total profits produced in the worldwide cell phone market.

"Steve understands desire," Alan Kay, a Xerox PARC pioneer who envisioned a "Dynabook" tablet computer forty years ago, remarked. Kay was known for his foresight, so Jobs asked him what he thought of the iPhone. "Make the screen five by eight inches, and you'll rule the world," Kay stated. He had no clue that the iPhone's design had begun with, and would eventually lead to, ideas for a tablet computer that would fulfil—indeed, exceed—his vision for the Dynabook.

CHAPTER 23

THE CANCER RECURS

Jobs and his physicians realised his illness was spreading by the beginning of 2008. When his pancreatic tumours were removed in 2004, the cancer genome was partially sequenced. This assisted his doctors in determining which pathways had been disrupted, and they were treating him with specific treatments that they believed were most likely to work. He was also being treated for pain, which was typically done with morphine-based painkillers. Powell and Jobs went for a walk one day in February 2008, while Powell's close friend Kathryn Smith was visiting with them in Palo Alto. "He told me that when he feels really bad, he just concentrates on the pain, goes into the pain, and that seems to dissipate it," she remembered. That wasn't entirely correct. When Jobs was in pain, he made it known to everyone around him. Another health concern became increasingly problematic, one that medical professionals did not study as thoroughly as cancer or pain. He was having trouble eating and was losing weight. This was due in part to the fact that he had lost much of his pancreas, which generates the enzymes required to digest protein and other nutrients. It was also due to the fact that both the cancer and the medication suppressed his appetite. Then there was the psychological aspect, which the doctors had no idea how to handle: He had indulged his strange infatuation with exceedingly tight diets and fasts from his early adolescence. He kept his questionable eating habits even after he married and had children. He'd eat the same item for weeks—carrot salad with lemon, or just apples—and then suddenly reject it and declare that he'd quit eating it. He'd go on fasts, just as he did when he was a youngster, and he'd get sanctimonious as he lectured people at the table on the advantages of whatever dietary regimen he was on. Powell had been a vegan when they first married, but following her husband's operation, she began to include fish and other proteins in their family dinners. Reed, their vegetarian kid, grew into a "hearty omnivore." They realised it was critical for his father to consume a variety of protein sources. Bryar Brown, a compassionate and skilled cook who formerly worked for Alice Waters at Chez Panisse, was hired by the family. He arrived every afternoon and prepared a variety of nutritious supper options using the herbs and vegetables Powell cultivated in their garden. Brown would quietly and painstakingly find a way to prepare whatever Jobs desired—carrot salad, pasta with basil, lemongrass soup. Jobs has always been a very opinionated eater, judging any cuisine as either wonderful or dreadful in an instant. He could taste two indistinguishable avocados and declare that one was the best avocado ever cultivated while the other was inedible.

Jobs' eating issues worsened beginning in early 2008. Some evenings, he would look at the floor, ignoring the dishes on the long kitchen table. He would get up and go without saying anything when others were halfway through their lunch. It was a difficult time for his family. During the spring of 2008, they watched him lose forty pounds. His health issues were brought to light again in March 2008, when Fortune published an article titled "The Trouble with Steve Jobs." It was discovered that he had tried to treat his cancer with diets for nine months and that he was also involved in the backdating of Apple stock options. Jobs summoned Fortune's managing editor Andy Serwer to Cupertino as the story was being prepared to pressure him to spike it. "So, you've discovered that I'm an asshole?" he questioned, leaning into Server's face. "What makes that news?" When Jobs called Server's employer at Time Inc., John Huey, via a satellite phone he took to Hawaii's Kona Village, he made the same pretty self-aware case. He promised to convene a panel of fellow CEOs to debate what health issues should be disclosed, but only if Fortune dropped its piece. The magazine, on the other hand, did not. Jobs was so skinny when he announced the iPhone 3G in June 2008 that it overshadowed the product unveiling. Tom Junod wrote in Esquire that the "withered" figure onstage was "gaunt as a pirate, dressed in what had heretofore been the vestments of his invulnerability." Apple issued a statement falsely claiming that his weight loss was caused by "a common bug." The following month, as questions persisted, the company released another statement saying that Jobs's health was "a private matter."

After a week filled with increasingly insistent legal advice, Jobs finally agreed to go on medical leave. George Fisher, a distinguished researcher on gastrointestinal and colorectal tumours at Stanford University, led Jobs' oncology team. He had been warning Jobs for months that he would need a liver transplant, but that was the type of information Jobs refused to accept. Powell was relieved that Fisher continued bringing up the topic, because she knew it would take several prod to get her husband to consider it. He was finally persuaded in January 2009, shortly after claiming that his "hormonal imbalance" could be readily addressed. But there was an issue. He was placed on a waiting list in California for a liver transplant, but it became evident that he would not receive one in time. There were few available donors with his blood type. Furthermore, the metrics employed by the United Network for Organ Sharing, which develops policies in the United States, preferred cirrhotic and hepatic patients over cancer patients. There is no legal way for a patient, even one as affluent as Jobs, to bypass the waiting list, and he did not do so. Recipients are chosen based on their MELD score (Model for End-Stage Liver Disease), which is determined by lab testing of hormone levels and the length of time they have been waiting. Every donation is carefully vetted, data is available on public websites (optn.transplant.hrsa.gov/), and you can check your waitlist status at any time. Powell became the organ-donation websites' troller, checking in every night to see how many people were on the waiting lists, what their MELD scores were, and how long they had been there. "You can do the maths, which I did, and it would have been way past June before he got a liver in California, and the doctors felt that his liver would give out in about April," she remembered. So she began asking questions and discovered that it was legal to be on the list in two different states at the same time, as approximately 3% of potential recipients do. Multiple listing is not discouraged by regulation, despite criticism that it advantages the wealthy, but it is difficult. There were two major prerequisites: The possible recipient had to be able to go to the chosen hospital within eight hours, which Jobs was able to do owing to his plane, and the doctors at that hospital had to assess the patient in person before adding him or her to the list. George Riley, the San Francisco attorney who frequently served as Apple's outside counsel, was a kind-hearted Tennessee gentleman who had grown close to Jobs. His parents were both doctors at Methodist University Hospital in Memphis, where he was born, and where he knew James Eason, who managed the transplant institute. Eason's unit was one of the best and busiest in the country, doing 121 liver transplants in 2008. He had no problem with persons from other cities multiple-listing in Memphis. "It's not a case of gaming the system," he remarked. "It is up to the people to decide where they want to receive their health care." Some folks might leave Tennessee to seek therapy in California or elsewhere. People are now travelling from California to Tennessee." Riley arranged for Season to fly to Palo Alto and complete the necessary assessment there. Jobs had acquired a spot on the Tennessee list (as well as the California list) by late February 2009, and the anxious waiting began. By the first week of March, he was fast deteriorating, and the waiting period was expected to be twenty-one days. "It was dreadful," Powell remembered. "It didn't appear that we'd make it in time." Every day grew more agonising. By mid-March, he had risen to third place, then second, and eventually first. But then time passed. The unfortunate reality was that impending events such as St. Patrick's Day and March Madness (Memphis was a regional location in the 2009 championship) increased the likelihood of finding a donor because drinking creates an increase in traffic accidents.

Indeed, on March 21, 2009, a young guy in his mid-twenties was murdered in a traffic accident, and his organs were donated. Jobs and his wife flew to Memphis, where they were welcomed by Eason shortly after landing. A car was waiting on the tarmac, and everything was set up so that they could complete the admission paperwork as they sped to the hospital. The transplant was successful, but it was not encouraging. When his liver was removed, physicians discovered spots on the peritoneum, the thin membrane that protects internal organs. Furthermore, there were tumours throughout the liver, implying that the cancer had spread elsewhere as well. It had obviously altered and expanded rapidly. They collected samples and performed additional genetic mapping. They needed to undergo another surgery a few days later. Jobs requested, against all advice, that his stomach not be pumped out, and while he was sedated, he inhaled part of the contents into his lungs and suffered pneumonia. They thought he was going to die at that point.

As he later explained, "I almost died because they blew it during this routine procedure." Laurene was there, and they flew my children in because they didn't think I'd survive the night. Reed and one of Laurene's brothers were looking at colleges. We had a private plane pick him up near Dartmouth and inform them of the situation. The girls were also picked up by plane. They felt it might be their last chance to see me awake. But I did it. Powell took care of the therapy, remaining in the hospital room all day and keeping a close eye on each of the monitors. "Laurene was a beautiful tiger protecting him," Jony Ive, who arrived as soon as Jobs was able to receive guests, recalls. Her mother and three brothers visited her at different times to keep her company. Mona Simpson, Jobs's sister, also stood guard. Jobs would only allow her and George Riley to stand in for Powell at his bedside. "Laurene's family helped us take care of the kids—her mom and brothers were great," Jobs later remarked. "I was extremely fragile and uncooperative." But an experience like that brings you closer together in a profound way."

Powell arrived at 7 a.m. every day and obtained the necessary data, which she entered into a spreadsheet. "It was very complicated because there were a lot of different things going on," she said. She would meet with James Eason and his team of doctors when they arrived at 9 a.m. to coordinate all elements of Jobs' treatment. Before she left at 9 p.m., she would compile a report on how each of the vital signs and other metrics were trending, as well as a list of questions she wanted answered the next day. "It allowed me to engage my brain and stay focused," she says.

Eason did something no one else at Stanford had done before: he took command of all elements of medical treatment. He was able to arrange transplant recovery, cancer tests, pain treatments, nourishment, rehabilitation, and nursing because he ran the facility. He'd even go to the convenience store to acquire the energy drinks Jobs preferred. Two of the nurses were from small Mississippi communities and quickly became Jobs' favourites. They were strong family ladies who were not scared by him. Eason made sure that they were solely assigned to Jobs. "To manage Steve, you have to be persistent," Tim Cook recalled. "Eason managed Steve and forced him to do things no one else could, things that were good for him but may not have been pleasant."

Despite all of the coddling, Jobs practically went insane at times. He was frustrated by his lack of control, and he occasionally hallucinated or grew enraged. His powerful personality shone through even when he was barely aware. When he was heavily sedated, the pulmonologist attempted to cover his face with a mask. Jobs took it off, muttering that he despised the design and refused to wear it. Despite his inability to talk, he instructed them to bring five different mask designs for him to choose from. Powell drew a perplexed glance from the doctors. She was finally able to divert his attention so that they could put on the mask. He also despised the oxygen monitor that was attached to his finger. He told them it was unattractive and overly complicated. He offered ideas to simplify the design. "He was very attuned to every nuance of his environment and the objects around him, and that drained him," Powell recalled.

Powell's close friend Kathryn Smith came to visit him one day while he was still floating in and out of consciousness. Her relationship with Jobs had not always been pleasant, but Powell insisted that she see Jobs in his hospital bed. He beckoned for her to come over, motioned for a pad and pen, and wrote, "I want my iPhone." Smith pulled it from the dresser and handed it to him. Taking her palm in his, he demonstrated the "swipe to open" function and made her experiment with the menus. Jobs' marriage to Lisa Brennan-Jobs, his daughter with Chrisann, had soured. She had graduated from Harvard, relocated to New York City, and had no contact with her father. She did, however, fly down to Memphis twice, which he liked. "It meant a lot to me that she would do that," he says. Regrettably, he did not inform her at the time. Many people surrounding Jobs thought Lisa was as demanding as her father, but Powell welcomed her and wanted to involve her. She wanted to repair the relationship. Much of Jobs' combative attitude resurfaced as he recovered. His bile ducts were still intact. "When he started to recover, he quickly passed through the phase of gratitude, and went right back into the mode of being grumpy and in charge," Kat Smith recounted. "We were all wondering if he was going to come out of this with a kinder perspective, but he didn't."

He was also still a picky eater, which was causing more problems than ever. He would only eat fruit smoothies, and he would demand that seven or eight of them be placed up for him to choose from. He'd put the spoon to his mouth for a tiny taste and say, "That's no good." That one is also a dud." Finally, Eason resisted. "You know, this isn't a matter of personal taste," he scolded. "Stop viewing this as food. Consider it to be medication."

Jobs' attitude improved when he had visits from Apple. Tim Cook comes down on a regular basis to update him on the status of new goods. "You could see him light up whenever the conversation turned to Apple," Cook added. "It was like the light turned on." He adored the company and appeared to live for the possibility of returning. He would be energised by specifics. When Cook detailed a new iPhone model, Jobs spent the next hour debating not just the name—they settled on iPhone 3GS—but also the size and typeface of the "GS," including whether the letters should be capitalised (yes) and italicised (no).

Riley organised for an after-hours surprise visit to Sun Studio, the redbrick shrine where Elvis Presley, Johnny Cash, B.B. King, and many other rock-and-roll pioneers recorded. One of the young staffers, who sat with Jobs on the cigarette-scarred bench that Jerry Lee Lewis used, gave them a private tour and history lesson. Jobs was undoubtedly the most powerful person in the music industry at the time, yet the gaunt child didn't identify him. Jobs said to Riley as they were leaving, "That kid was really smart." He should work for iTunes." So Riley contacted Eddy Cue, who flew the lad up to California for an interview and eventually hired him to help construct iTunes' early R&B and rock-and-roll sections. Riley afterwards returned to Sun Studio to meet his pals, who noted that it proved, as their tagline stated, that your dreams can still come true at Sun Studio.

CHAPTER 24

THE iPAD

Jobs was irritated in 2002 by a Microsoft developer who kept evangelising about the tablet computer software he had built, which allowed users to input information on the screen using a stylus or pen. A few manufacturers developed tablet PCs using the software that year, but none had a significant impact on the market. Jobs was anxious to demonstrate how it should be done correctly—no stylus!—but when he saw the multi-touch technology that Apple was developing, he opted to use it first to create the iPhone. Meanwhile, the tablet concept was circulating among the Macintosh hardware team. "We have no plans to make a tablet," Jobs stated in a May 2003 interview with Walt Mossberg. "It turns out that people like keyboards. Tablets appeal to wealthy men who already have a plethora of PCs and devices." That, like his claim about having a "hormone imbalance," was deceptive; at the majority of his yearly Top 100 retreats, the tablet was among the future projects addressed. "We showed the idea off at many of these retreats, because Steve never lost his desire to do a tablet," Phil Schiller recounted. When Jobs was investigating ideas for a low-cost netbook computer in 2007, he gave the tablet project a boost. One Monday, at an executive team brainstorming session, I queried why it needed a keyboard hinged to the screen; it was pricey and cumbersome. He recommended putting the keyboard on the screen using a multi-touch interface. Jobs concurred. As a result, rather than building a netbook, resources were put on accelerating the tablet project. The process began with Jobs and I've determined the appropriate screen size. They had twenty models produced, all rounded rectangles of varied sizes and aspect ratios. I'd placed them out on a table in the design studio, and they'd lift the velvet cloth that was hiding them and play with them in the afternoon. "That's how we nailed down what the screen size was," I've explained.

Jobs, as usual, pushed for the utmost simplicity. This necessitated determining the device's basic nature. The display screen is the answer. As a result, the driving idea was that everything they did had to be based on the screen. "How do we get out of the way so that there aren't a bunch of features and buttons distracting from the display?" I inquired. Jobs pushed for removal and simplification at every turn. Jobs was mildly dissatisfied with the model at one point. It didn't feel casual or welcoming enough for you to naturally grab it up and whisk it away. I've pointed his finger at the problem: They needed to indicate that you could take it with one hand on the spur of the moment. The bottom of the edge needs to be slightly rounded so that you could scoop it up rather than carefully raising it. That meant engineers had to construct the necessary connection ports and buttons onto a simple lip thin enough to wash away softly beneath. If you had been keeping track of patent filings, you would have spotted the one numbered D504889, which Apple applied for in March 2004 and received fourteen months later. Jobs and Ive were among the inventors named. The application included illustrations of a rectangular electronic tablet with rounded corners that resembled the iPad, including one of a man holding it casually in his left hand while touching the screen with his right index finger. Because Macintosh machines were now using Intel chips, Jobs planned to employ the low-voltage Atom CPU that Intel was creating in the iPad. Intel's CEO, Paul Otellini, was pressuring them to collaborate on a design, and Jobs was inclined to believe him. His company was producing the world's fastest processors. However, Intel was accustomed to producing processors for computers that plugged into a wall, not those that needed to conserve battery life. As a result, Tony Fadell lobbied hard for something based on the ARM architecture, which was simpler and required less power. Apple was an early partner with ARM, and chips based on its architecture were used in the first iPhone. Fadell enlisted the help of other engineers and demonstrated that it was feasible to face Jobs and turn him around. "Wrong, wrong, and wrong!" When Jobs insisted on trusting Intel to build a good mobile chip, Fadell yelled during one meeting. Fadell even threatened to resign by placing his Apple credential on the table. Jobs eventually succumbed. "I hear you," he admitted. "I'm not going to face off against my best guys." In reality, he went the other way. Apple licensed the ARM architecture, but it also purchased P.A. Semi, a 150-person microprocessor design firm in Palo Alto, and had it construct a unique system-on-a-chip called the A4, which was based on the ARM architecture and built by Samsung in South Korea. According to Jobs, Intel is the greatest at high-performance computing. If you don't care about power or cost, they make the fastest chip. However, because they only create the processor on one chip, many other parts are required. Our A4 includes the processor, graphics, mobile operating system, and memory control all on a single chip. We attempted to assist Intel, but they were unresponsive. For years, we've been warning them that their visuals are terrible. We have a quarterly meeting with me, our top three guys, and Paul Otellini. We were doing fantastic things together at first. They desired this large collaborative initiative to produce semiconductors for future iPhones. We didn't go with them for two reasons. One was that they are simply extremely slow. They're not as adaptable as a steamship. We're used to moving quickly. The second reason was that we didn't want to teach them everything, which they could then sell to our competitors. It would have made sense, according to Otellini, for the iPad to use Intel CPUs. He claimed that the issue was that Apple and Intel couldn't agree on pricing. They also argued on who would be in charge of the design. It exemplified Jobs' ambition, no, compulsion, to control every part of a product, from the silicon to the flesh. The normal fervour Steve Jobs could generate for a product launch paled in comparison to the hysteria that erupted for the iPad's introduction on January 27, 2010, in San Francisco. The Economist featured him on its cover, robed and haloed, carrying what became known as "the Jesus Tablet." According to the Wall Street Journal, "the last time there was this much excitement about a tablet, it had some commandments written on it."

To emphasise the historic nature of the event, Jobs invited several of his early Apple colleagues back. More poignantly, James Eason, who had received a liver transplant the previous year, and Jeffrey Norton, who had undergone pancreas surgery in 2004, were in the crowd, sitting with his wife, son, and Mona Simpson. Jobs did his customary masterful job of contextualising a new technology, as he had done three years previously with the iPhone. This time, he displayed an iPhone and a laptop with a question mark in between. "The question is, is there room for something in the middle?" he inquired. That "something" must be capable of web browsing, email, photographs, video, music, games, and ebooks. He put a spike through the netbook concept's heart. He said, "Netbooks aren't better at anything!" Employees and invited guests applauded. "However, we have something that is. It's known as the iPad."

To emphasise the iPad's casual character, Jobs strolled over to a nice leather chair and side table (really, given his taste, it was a Le Corbusier chair and an Eero Saarinen table) and grabbed one up. "It's so much more intimate than a laptop," he said. He went on to browse the New York Times website, send an email to Scott Forstall and Phil Schiller ("Wow, we really are announcing the iPad"), flip through a photo album, use a calendar, zoom in on the Eiffel Tower on Google Maps, watch some video clips (Star Trek and Pixar's Up), show off the iBook shelf, and play a song (Bob Dylan's "Like a Rolling Stone," which he played at the iPhone launch). "Isn't that awesome?" he exclaimed. Jobs' final slide underlined one of his life's themes, which was encapsulated by the iPad: a sign depicting the intersection of Technology Street and Liberal Arts Street. "The reason Apple can create products like the iPad is that we've always tried to be at the intersection of technology and liberal arts," he said. The iPad was the digital incarnation of the Whole Earth Catalog, where creativity met living instruments.

For the first time, there was no Hallelujah Chorus. The iPad was not yet available (it will be on sale in April), and some viewers were perplexed by Jobs' demonstration. An iPhone on speed? "I haven't been this let down since Snooki hooked up with The Situation," Newsweek's Daniel Lyons (who also moonlighted as "The Fake Steve Jobs" in an online parody) remarked. Gizmodo published an article by a contributor titled "Eight Things That Suck About the iPad" (no multitasking, no cameras, no Flash...). Even the name was mocked in the blogosphere, with snide remarks about feminine hygiene items and maxi pads. The hashtag "#iTampon" was the third most popular subject on Twitter that day. There was also the obligatory rebuke from Bill Gates. "I still believe that some combination of voice, pen, and real keyboard—that is, a netbook—will be the mainstream," he told Brent Schlender. "So it's not like I sit there and think, 'Oh my God, Microsoft didn't aim high enough,' like I did with the iPhone." It's a wonderful reader, but there's nothing else on the iPad that makes me think, 'Oh, I wish Microsoft had done it.'" He insisted that the Microsoft strategy of using a pen for input would be successful. "I've been predicting a tablet with a stylus for many years," he admitted. "I will either prove to be correct or die."

Jobs was irritated and depressed the night after his announcement. As we sat down for dinner in his kitchen, he strolled around the table, pulling up emails and site pages on his iPhone. In the previous twenty-four hours, I received approximately 800 email messages. Most of them are whining. There is no USB cable! There is no such thing as this or that. "Fuck you, how can you do that?" several of them say. I don't normally respond to emails, but I did say, "Your parents would be so proud of how you turned out." And some people dislike the iPad name, and so on. Today I became a little depressed. It takes you aback a little. That day, he did receive a congratulatory call from President Obama's chief of staff, Rahm Emanuel, which he appreciated. He did, however, mention during dinner that the president had not called him since assuming office. When the iPad went on sale in April and consumers got their hands on it, the public outcry faded. It was featured on the covers of Time and Newsweek. "The tough thing about writing about Apple products is that they come with a lot of hype wrapped around them," Time's Lev Grossman wrote. "Another difficult aspect of writing about Apple products is that sometimes the hype is true." His biggest qualm was that "while it's a lovely device for consuming content, it doesn't do much to facilitate its creation." Computers, particularly the Macintosh, had evolved into tools that enabled people to create music, videos, websites, and blogs that could be shared with the rest of the world. "With the iPad, the emphasis shifts from creating content to simply absorbing and manipulating it." It silences you, reverting you to a passive consumer of other people's works." Jobs took the criticism to heart. He set about ensuring that the future edition of the iPad would focus techniques to facilitate the user's artistic work.

In less than a month Apple sold one million iPads. That was twice as fast as it took the iPhone to reach that mark. By March 2011, nine months after its release, fifteen million had been sold. By some measures it became the most successful consumer product launch in history.

CHAPTER 25

NEW BATTLES

Jobs hosted a "town hall" meeting with Apple employees a few days after unveiling the iPad in January 2010. Instead of celebrating their game-changing new device, he went on a rant against Google for creating the competing Android operating system. Jobs was enraged when Google started to compete with Apple in the phone market. "We did not enter the search business," he explained. "They got into the phone business." Make no doubt about it. They aim to destroy the iPhone. We're not going to let them." After the discussion had moved on to another topic, Jobs resumed his tirade against Google's famed values motto. "First, I'd like to return to that other question and say one more thing." This 'Don't be bad' motto is nonsense."

Jobs felt violated personally. Google CEO Eric Schmidt served on Apple's board of directors during the creation of the iPhone and iPad, and Google's founders, Larry Page and Sergey Brin, looked up to him as a mentor. He felt taken advantage of. Android's touchscreen interface was incorporating more and more of Apple's features, such as multi-touch, swiping, and a grid of app icons. Jobs had attempted to persuade Google not to build Android. In 2008, he went to Google's headquarters outside Palo Alto and got into an argument with Page, Brin, and Andy Rubin, the head of the Android development team. (Because Schmidt was on the Apple board at the time, he recused himself from iPhone talks.) "I said that if we had good relations, we would guarantee Google access to the iPhone and one or two icons on the home screen," he recalled. He also threatened to sue Google if it continued to develop Android and exploited any iPhone features, such as multi-touch. Google initially avoided replicating specific features, but in January 2010, HTC released an Android phone with multi-touch and many other capabilities similar to the iPhone's appearance and feel. That was the setting in which Jobs declared that Google's "Don't be evil" slogan was "bullshit."

So Apple sued HTC (and, by extension, Android) for infringement of twenty of its patents. Patents covering numerous multi-touch motions, such as swipe to open, double-tap to zoom, pinch and expand, and sensors that sensed how a device was handled, were among them. He got angrier than I had ever seen him the week the case was filed, sitting at his Palo Alto home: "Google, you fucking ripped off the iPhone, wholesale ripped us off." Theft on a grand scale. If necessary, I will spend my last dying breath, as well as every penny of Apple's $40 billion in the bank, to right this wrong. Android will be destroyed because it is a stolen product. On this, I'm willing to go to nuclear war. They are terrified because they know they are guilty. Aside from Search, Google's products—Android and Google Docs—are abysmal. A few days after this rant, Jobs received a call from Schmidt, who had resigned from Apple's board of directors the previous summer. He recommended they meet for coffee, and they did so at a café in a Palo Alto shopping mall. "We spent half the time talking about personal matters, then half the time talking about his perception that Google had stolen Apple's user interface designs," Schmidt remembered. When it came to the latter, Jobs did the majority of the talking. He used colourful words to describe how Google had taken advantage of him. "We've got you caught red-handed," he said to Schmidt. "I'm not looking to settle. I'm not interested in your money. If you offer me $5 billion, I will decline. I have a lot of money. All I ask is that you cease utilising our concepts in Android." They made no progress. Underlying the conflict was a more fundamental issue, one with unsettling historical significance. Google marketed Android as an "open" platform, with open-source code freely available for use on whatever phones or tablets were created. Jobs, of course, was adamant that Apple's operating systems and hardware be tightly integrated. Apple did not licence out its Macintosh operating system in the 1980s, and Microsoft eventually won overwhelming market share by licensing its system to many device makers and, in Jobs' opinion, ripping off Apple's interface. The parallel between what Microsoft accomplished in the 1980s and what Google attempted in 2010 was not exact, but it was similar enough to be unsettling—and furious. It typified the big digital-age debate: closed vs open, or, as Jobs put it, integrated against fragmented. Was it better, as Apple claimed and as Jobs' own controlling perfectionism nearly required, to integrate hardware, software, and content management into a single clean system that guaranteed a straightforward user experience? Or was it better to provide consumers and manufacturers more options while also opening up new avenues for creativity by developing software systems that could be changed and used on a variety of devices? "Steve has a particular way he wants to run Apple, and it's the same as it was twenty years ago, which is that Apple is a brilliant innovator of closed systems," Schmidt explained afterwards. "They don't want people using their platform without their permission." Control is one of the advantages of a closed platform. However, Google believes that being open is the superior strategy since it leads to more options, competition, and consumer choice."

So, what did Bill Gates think when he watched Jobs, with his closed approach, go into a fight against Google, as he had done twenty-five years previously against Microsoft? "There are some benefits to being more closed, in terms of how much control you have over the experience, and certainly at times he's had the benefit of that," Gates explained. However, he said that declining to licence Apple's iOS provided competitors such as Android the opportunity to acquire market share. Furthermore, he contended that rivalry among various devices and producers leads to increased consumer choice and innovation. "These companies are not all building pyramids next to Central Park," he said, referring to Apple's Fifth Avenue location, "but they are coming up with innovations based on competing for consumers." The majority of advancements in PCs, according to Gates, occurred because users had a wide range of options, which would someday be the situation in the realm of mobile devices. "I believe that open will eventually succeed, but that is where I come from." In the long run, the coherence issue cannot be sustained."

Jobs was a firm believer in "the coherence thing." Even as Android gained market dominance, his trust in a controlled and restricted environment remained strong. "Google says we have more control than they do, that we are closed and they are open," he raged when I informed him of Schmidt's comments. "Look at the results—Android is a shambles." It contains nearly a hundred combinations of screen sizes and versions." Even if Google's approach finally prevailed in the marketplace, Jobs found it repulsive. "I enjoy being in charge of the entire user experience." We don't do it for the money. We do it because we want to create wonderful goods rather than garbage like Android."

Jobs' insistence on total control was also evident in other disputes. He slammed Adobe's multimedia framework for websites, Flash, as a "buggy" battery hog created by "lazy" people at the town hall gathering where he lambasted Google. He said that Flash will never operate on the iPod or iPhone. "Flash is a spaghetti-ball piece of technology with poor performance and serious security issues," he told me later that week. He even barred apps that used Adobe's compiler, which transformed Flash code to make it compatible with Apple's iOS. Jobs despised the use of compilers, which allowed developers to write once and have their products ported to many operating systems. "Allowing Flash to be ported across platforms means that things get dumbed down to the lowest common denominator," he explained. "We put in a lot of effort to improve our platform, and the developer loses out if Adobe only works with functions that every platform has." As a result, we stated that we want developers to take advantage of our superior features, so that their apps operate better on our platform than on anybody else's." He was correct in that regard. Losing Apple's capacity to differentiate its platforms, enabling them to become commoditized like HP and Dell machines, would have meant the company's demise. There was also a more personal motivation. In 1985, Apple invested in Adobe, and the two businesses collaborated to begin the desktop publishing revolution. "I helped put Adobe on the map," Jobs asserted. After returning to Apple in 1999, Jobs requested Adobe to begin producing video editing software and other goods for the iMac and its new operating system, but Adobe refused. It concentrated on developing products for Windows. John Warnock, the company's founder, retired soon after. "When Warnock left, the soul of Adobe vanished," Jobs observed. "He was the inventor, the person to whom I related." Since then, there have been a slew of cases, and the corporation has produced mediocre results."

When Adobe evangelists and other Flash supporters attacked Jobs on the blogosphere for being excessively controlling, he decided to write and post an open letter. Bill Campbell, a friend and board member, dropped by to discuss it. "Does it sound like I'm just trying to stick it to Adobe?" he wondered. "No, it's facts, just put it out there," responded the coach. The majority of the letter focused on Flash's technological shortcomings. Despite Campbell's coaching, Jobs couldn't help but rant at the conclusion about the two firms' tumultuous history. "Adobe was the last major third-party developer to fully adopt Mac OS X," he pointed out.

Later in the year, Apple relaxed some of its restrictions on cross-platform compilers, allowing Adobe to release a Flash creation tool that made advantage of important capabilities of Apple's iOS. It was a hard battle, but Jobs had the superior argument. Finally, it encouraged Adobe and other compiler developers to make better use of the iPhone and iPad interface and particular features. Jobs struggled to navigate the difficulties surrounding Apple's determination to maintain strict control over which apps could be put onto the iPhone and iPad. Protecting against apps that contained viruses or abused the user's privacy made sense; prohibiting apps that directed users to other websites to purchase subscriptions rather than the iTunes Store had a financial purpose. But Jobs and his colleagues went much further, deciding to block any program that defamed people, could be politically combustible, or was deemed sexual by Apple's censors. The issue of playing nanny became clear when Apple rejected an app including Mark Fiore's animated political cartoons, claiming that his attacks on the Bush administration's torture policies breached the rule against defamation. When Fiore won the 2010 Pulitzer Prize for editorial cartooning in April, the choice became public and was mocked. Apple was forced to backtrack, and Jobs issued a public apology. "We're both guilty of making mistakes," he admitted. "We're doing the best we can, learning as fast as we can—but we thought this rule made sense."

It was more than a blunder. It posed the prospect of Apple dictating which apps we could see and read if we wanted to use an iPad or iPhone. Jobs appeared to be on the verge of becoming the Orwellian Big Brother he had gleefully demolished in Apple's "1984" Macintosh commercial. He was concerned about the situation. He phoned New York Times columnist Tom Friedman one day to talk about how to draw borders without looking like a censor. He invited Friedman to chair an advisory council to assist develop rules, but the columnist's publisher refused, citing a conflict of interest, and no such committee was formed. The ban on pornography also produced issues. "We believe we have a moral responsibility to keep porn off the iPhone," Jobs stated in a customer email. "Those looking for porn can get an Android."

This sparked an email conversation with Ryan Tate, the editor of the tech gossip website Valleywag. Tate, while sipping a stinger cocktail one evening, sent Jobs an email criticising Apple's heavy-handed supervision over which programs passed approval. "If Dylan was 20 today, how would he feel about your company?" Tate inquired. "Would he believe the iPad has anything to do with revolution'? "Revolutions are about achieving freedom."

Jobs responded a few hours later, around midnight, much to Tate's amazement. "Yep," he responded, "freedom from programs that steal your personal information." Freedom from battery-depleting programs. The absence of porn. Yes, liberty. The times they are a-changin', and some conventional PC types feel as if their world is crumbling around them. It is."

Tate responded with some views on Flash and other issues before returning to the censorship issue. "And you know what else? I'm not interested in 'freedom from porn.' Porn is perfectly acceptable! And I believe my wife would concur."

"You might care more about porn when you have kids," Jobs responded. "It's not about liberty; it's about Apple doing the right thing for its customers." He finished with a zinger: "By the way, what have you done that is so great?" Do you make anything or merely criticise and dismiss the efforts of others?"

Tate stated that he was amazed. "Rare is the CEO who will spar one-on-one with customers and bloggers like this," he wrote. "Jobs deserves a lot of credit for breaking the mould of the typical American executive, and not just because his company produces such vastly superior products: Jobs not only built and then rebuilt his company around some very strong opinions about digital life, but he's willing to defend them publicly." Vigorously. Bluntly. On a Sunday morning at two a.m." Many bloggers agreed, and many wrote Jobs emails admiring his tenacity. Jobs was also pleased; he forwarded his conversation with Tate and some of the compliments to me. Still, Apple's directive that consumers who purchased their goods refrain from viewing provocative political cartoons or erotica was unsettling. Jobs and Apple were at the time embroiled in a legal battle with Valleywag's connected website, Gizmodo, which had obtained a test version of the unannounced iPhone 4 that a careless Apple engineer had left in a bar. When the police raided the reporter's house in response to Apple's complaint, it raised the question of whether control freakiness had mingled with arrogance.

Jobs' friend and Apple lover was Jon Stewart. Jobs had paid him a secret visit in February during his trip to New York to meet with media leaders. Stewart, on the other hand, went after him on The Daily Show. "This wasn't meant to happen! Microsoft was supposed to be the bad guy!" Stewart joked half-heartedly. The word "appholes" showed on the screen behind him. "Man, you guys were the rebels, the underdogs. But are you now becoming The Man? Remember those amazing ads about overthrowing Big Brother back in 1984? "Man, look in the mirror!"

By late spring, board members were debating the problem. "There is an arrogance," Art Levinson told me over lunch, shortly after bringing it up in a meeting. "It has something to do with Steve's personality." He has the ability to react viscerally and forcefully express his convictions." Such hubris was acceptable when Apple was the tenacious underdog. However, Apple now dominated the smartphone market. "We need to transition to being a large company and deal with the hubris issue," Levinson remarked. At board meetings, Al Gore also addressed the issue. "The context for Apple is changing dramatically," he says. "This isn't a hammer-thrower versus Big Brother. Now that Apple is big, some regard it as arrogant." When the subject was brought up, Jobs became defensive. "He's still adjusting to it," Gore explained. "He's better at being the underdog than a humble giant."

Jobs had little time for such nonsense. He explained that Apple was being targeted because "companies like Google and Adobe are lying about us and trying to tear us down." What did he make of the idea that Apple acted arrogantly at times? "I'm not worried about that," he explained, "because we're not arrogant."

In many consumer product companies, there is conflict between designers who want to make a product seem attractive and engineers who need to ensure it meets its practical needs. That tension was amplified at Apple, where Jobs pushed both design and engineering to their limits. When he and design director Jony Ive first collaborated on a project in 1997, they saw engineers' reservations as evidence of a can't-do attitude that needed to be addressed. The success of the iMac and iPod strengthened their belief that awesome design might induce superhuman feats of engineering. When engineers indicated something couldn't be done, Ive and Jobs pushed them to try, and most of the time they were successful. There were a few minor issues. Because I've considered that a transparent coating would impair the purity of his design, the iPod Nano, for example, was prone to scratching. That, however, was hardly a crisis.

When it came to designing the iPhone, Ive's design aspirations collided with a fundamental law of physics that could not be altered even by a reality distortion field. Metal should not be placed near an antenna. Electromagnetic waves, as demonstrated by Michael Faraday, pass around the surface of metal rather than through it. A metal enclosure surrounding a phone, for example, can produce a Faraday cage, reducing the amount of signal that gets in or out. The original iPhone had a plastic ring at the bottom, but I've decided that would ruin the design and asked for an aluminium rim all around. After it proved successful, I designed the iPhone 4 with a steel rim. The steel would be the structural support, as well as a component of the phone's antenna.There were substantial difficulties. The steel rim required a slight gap in order to function as an antenna. However, if a person covers that gap with a finger or sweaty palm, some signal loss may occur. To help prevent this, the engineers suggested a clear covering over the metal, but I believed that this would detract from the brushed-metal aesthetic. The problem was brought up to Jobs at several meetings, but he dismissed it as engineers crying wolf. He said, "You can make this work." That is exactly what they did. And it worked almost flawlessly. However, not completely. When the iPhone 4 was released in June 2010, it looked fantastic, but there was a problem: if you held the phone in a specific way, particularly with your left hand such that your palm covered the tiny gap, you could lose your connection. It happened around once per hundred calls. Because Jobs was adamant about keeping his unreleased products hidden (even the phone Gizmodo found in a pub had a phoney case around it), the iPhone 4 did not go through the live testing that other electronic gadgets do. As a result, the problem was not discovered before the tremendous rush to purchase it began. "The question is whether Apple benefited from the twin policies of putting design ahead of engineering and having a policy of supersecrecy surrounding unreleased products," Tony Fadell subsequently commented. "On the whole, yes," says the author, "but unchecked power is a bad thing, and that's what happened."

The issue of a few extra dropped calls would not have made headlines if it hadn't been for the Apple iPhone 4, a device that had everyone's attention. But it became known as "Antennagate," and it came to a climax in early July, when Consumer Reports conducted rigorous tests and stated that the iPhone 4 could not be recommended due to the antenna problem. Jobs was with his family in Kona Village, Hawaii, when the problem began. He was initially defensive. Art Levinson was in frequent phone contact with Jobs, who stated that the problem was caused by Google and Motorola misbehaving. "They want to shoot Apple down," he explained.

Levinson encouraged some humility. "Let's try to figure out if there's something wrong," he remarked. Jobs was irritated when he was reminded of the idea that Apple was arrogant. It contradicted his black-and-white, right-and-wrong worldview. He thought Apple was a principled company. If others didn't notice it, it was their problem, not Apple's, and it's not a reason for Apple to be modest. Jobs' second reaction was one of pain. He took the comments personally and became distraught. "At his core, he doesn't do things that he thinks are blatantly wrong, like some pure pragmatists in our business," Levinson explained. "So, if he believes he is correct, he will charge ahead rather than question himself." Levinson advised him not to become depressed. However, Jobs did. "Fuck this, it's not worth it," he exclaimed to Levinson. Finally, Tim Cook was able to rouse him from his slumber. According to him, Apple is becoming the new Microsoft, complacent and arrogant. Jobs' attitude shifted the next day. "Let's get to the bottom of this," he remarked, addressing the audience. When AT&T data on dropped calls was compiled, Jobs acknowledged there was a problem, even if it was less serious than people made it out to be. As a result, he flew back from Hawaii. He did, however, make a few phone calls before leaving. It was time to call in a pair of trustworthy old hands, wise individuals who had been with him from the early days of the Macintosh thirty years before. His first contact was to public relations guru Regis McKenna. "I'm coming back from Hawaii to deal with this antenna thing, and I need to bounce some stuff off of you," Jobs explained. They arranged to meet the next afternoon at 1:30 in the Cupertino boardroom. The second call was to advertising executive Lee Clow. He had attempted to leave the Apple account, but Jobs preferred to keep him around. His colleague James Vincent was also summoned.

Jobs also opted to bring his son Reed, a high school senior at the time, back from Hawaii. "I'm going to be in meetings 24/7 for probably two days, and I want you to be in every single one because you'll learn more in those two days than you would in two years at business school," he explained. "You're going to be in a room with the best people in the world making really tough decisions, and you'll get to see how the sausage is made." When he recalled the encounter, Jobs became teary-eyed. "I would go through it all over again just to have him see me at work," he said. "He got to see what his dad does."

Katie Cotton, Apple's solid public relations chief, and seven other top executives joined them. The meeting lasted the entire afternoon. "It was one of the greatest meetings of my life," Jobs recalled afterwards. He began by listing all of the information they had gathered. "The facts are as follows. So, what are we going to do about it?" McKenna was the most composed and direct. "Just lay it out there, the truth, the data," he remarked. "Don't appear arrogant, but firm and confident." Others, notably Vincent, pressed Jobs to be more contrite, but McKenna refused. "Don't go into the press conference with your tail between your legs," he recommended. "You should just say, 'Phones aren't perfect, and neither are we.'" We're human, doing our best, and here's the evidence." That became the plan. When the conversation shifted to the perception of arrogance, McKenna advised him not to be too concerned. "I don't think it would work to try to make Steve look humble," McKenna subsequently added. "As Steve says about himself, 'What you see is what you get.'" Jobs took McKenna's advice and staged the press presentation that Friday in Apple's auditorium. He did not grovel or apologise, but he was able to diffuse the situation by demonstrating that Apple recognized the situation and would work to make it right. Then he shifted the conversation's focus, claiming that all cell phones had flaws. Later, he informed me that he had sounded "too annoyed" during the event, but in reality, he was able to establish an unemotional and plain tone. "We're not perfect," he said in four short, straightforward terms. Phones are not without flaws. That is something we are all aware of. But we aim to please our customers."

If customers were dissatisfied, he noted, they could return the phone (the return rate was 1.7%, less than a third of the return rate for the iPhone 3GS or most other phones) or get a free bumper cover from Apple. He went on to present statistics indicating that other mobile phones experienced similar issues. That was not entirely correct. Because of Apple's antenna design, it performed slightly poorer than most other phones, including previous generations of the iPhone. However, the media hysteria over the iPhone 4's dropped calls was exaggerated. "This has been blown out of proportion so much that it's incredible," he remarked. Instead of being outraged that he didn't apologise or force a recall, most people acknowledged he was correct. The phone's already-sold-out wait list was extended from two to three weeks. It remained the company's best-selling product of all time. The media argument switched to whether Jobs was correct in asserting that other smartphones had the same antenna issues. Even if the answer was no, it was a better story to tell than whether the iPhone 4 was a faulty dud. There were a few issues that needed to be fixed before Steve Jobs' career could be considered complete. Among them was the end of the Thirty Years' War with his favourite band, the Beatles. In 2007, Apple settled its trademark dispute with Apple Corps, the holding company of the Beatles, who had sued the embryonic computer business in 1978 over the use of the name. However, the Beatles were still not accepted into the iTunes Store. The band was the final major holdout, owing to an impasse with EMI music, who controlled the majority of its songs, over how to handle digital rights. By the summer of 2010, the Beatles and EMI had settled their differences, and a four-person summit was conducted in Cupertino's boardroom. Jobs and his vice president for the iTunes Store, Eddy Cue, hosted Jeff Jones, the Beatles' manager, and Roger Faxon, the head of EMI music. What could Apple give to make the Beatles' digital debut special now that they were ready? Jobs had been looking forward to this day for a long time. In reality, he and his advertising team, Lee Clow and James Vincent, had sketched up some ads and commercials three years earlier while planning how to entice the Beatles to join them.

"Steve and I discussed everything we could possibly do," Cue recalled. This includes taking over the top page of the iTunes Store, purchasing billboards showing the band's greatest images, and airing a series of television commercials in traditional Apple flair. The top seller was a $149 box set that featured all thirteen Beatles studio albums, the two-volume "Past Masters" collection, and a film of the 1964 Washington Coliseum concert. After they reached an agreement in principle, Jobs personally assisted in the selection of pictures for the advertisements. Each commercial concluded with a black-and-white image of Paul McCartney and John Lennon, both young and smiling, in a recording studio, looking down at a piece of music. It reminded me of old photos of Jobs and Wozniak inspecting an Apple circuit board. "Getting the Beatles on iTunes was the pinnacle of why we got into the music business," Cue explained.

CHAPTER 26

TO INFINITY

Even before the iPad was released, Jobs was considering what will be included in the iPad 2. Everyone expected it to have front and rear cameras, and he obviously wanted it to be slimmer. But there was a side issue that he concentrated on that most people hadn't considered: People's cases obscured the iPad's attractive lines and detracted from the screen. They made what should be thinner and fatter. They put a mundane cloak on a gadget that should be miraculous in every way. He cut out an article about magnets and handed it to Jony Ive around that time. The magnets possessed a precise cone of attraction that could be targeted. They could also be used to align a detachable cover. It could then snap onto the front of an iPad without engulfing the entire device. One of Ive's group members devised a way to construct a detachable cover that could connect using a magnetic hinge. When you started to open it, the screen would light up like a tickling baby's face, and the cover would fold into a stand. It was entirely mechanical, not high-tech. It was, nevertheless, wonderful. It was also another evidence of Jobs' ambition for end-to-end integration: the cover and the iPad had been built in tandem, with the magnets and hinge all flawlessly integrated. The iPad 2 would have numerous upgrades, but it was this cheeky little cover, which most other CEOs would never bother with, that would elicit the most chuckles. Jobs was not expected to attend the iPad 2 premiere on March 2, 2011, in San Francisco, because he was on another medical leave. However, when the invites were sent out, he informed me that I should make an effort to go. It was the traditional scene: senior Apple executives in the front row, Tim Cook eating energy bars, and the sound system blasting appropriate Beatles tunes, gradually building up to "Revolution" and "Here Comes the Sun." Reed Jobs showed up at the last minute, accompanied by two fairly wide-eyed freshman dorm mates.

"We've been working on this product for a while, and I just didn't want to miss today," Jobs remarked as he ambled onstage, scarily gaunt but smiling. The audience responded with whoops, hollers, and a standing ovation.

He began his iPad 2 demo by displaying the new cover. "This time, the case and the product were designed together," he says. Then he addressed a critique that had been bothering him because it had some merit: The first iPad was better at consuming material than it was at creating it. As a result, Apple updated its two finest creative applications for the Macintosh, GarageBand and iMovie, and made powerful iPad versions available. Jobs demonstrated how simple it was to compose and orchestrate a song, or to incorporate music and special effects into home films, and then to broadcast or share such compositions using the new iPad. He concluded his presentation once more with a graphic depicting the crossroads of Liberal Arts Street and Technology Street. And this time, he gave one of the clearest expressions of his credo, that true creativity and simplicity come from integrating the entire widget—hardware and software, as well as content, covers, and sales clerks—rather than allowing things to be open and fragmented, as happened with Windows PCs and is now happening with Android devices: It's in Apple's DNA that technology alone is not enough. We believe that technology combined with the humanities produces the product that makes our hearts sing. That is especially true in these post-PC gadgets. People are racing into the tablet market, viewing it as the next PC, with hardware and software developed by separate companies. That is not the appropriate method, according to our experience and every bone in our body. These are post-PC devices that must be more intuitive and easier to use than a PC, and where software, hardware, and applications must be integrated in a more fluid manner than on a PC. We believe we have the necessary architecture to produce these kinds of goods, not just in silicon, but also in our company. It was an architecture nurtured not only into the institution he had created, but also into his own spirit. Jobs was pumped after the launch event. He came to the Four Seasons hotel for lunch with me, his wife, Reed, and Reed's two Stanford buddies. He was eating for the first time in a long time, albeit he was still picky. He requested fresh-squeezed juice, which he returned three times, claiming that each new delivery was from a bottle, and spaghetti primavera, which he tossed aside after one taste as inedible. He ate half of my crab Louie salad and then ordered a whole one for himself, followed by a bowl of ice cream. The opulent hotel even produced a glass of juice that satisfied his exacting demands. He was still high the next day when I arrived at his residence. I asked him what he had on his iPad 2 for the trip because he was flying to Kona Village alone the next day. Chinatown, The Bourne Ultimatum, and Toy Story 3 were the three films. More interesting, he had only downloaded one book: The Autobiography of a Yogi, a meditation and spirituality guide that he had first read as a youth, then reread in India, and had read once a year ever since. He decided to eat something midway through the morning. I drove him to a café in a shopping mall because he was still too weak to drive. It was closed, but the owner was used to Jobs pounding on the door after hours, so he let us in. "He's set out on a mission to fatten me up," Jobs said. His physicians had advised him to eat eggs as a high-quality protein source, so he ordered an omelette. "Living with a disease like this, with all the pain, constantly reminds you of your own mortality, and that can do strange things to your brain if you're not careful," he explained. "You don't plan more than a year ahead, which is bad. You must force yourself to plan as if you will live for a long time."

His plan to create a magnificent yacht was an illustration of his magical thinking. He and his family used to hire a yacht for trips to Mexico, the South Pacific, or the Mediterranean before his liver transplant. Jobs became bored or disliked the design of the boat on many of these trips, so they would cut the trip short and fly to Kona Village. However, the cruise did work occasionally. "The best vacation I've ever been on was when we went down the coast of Italy, then to Athens—which is a pit, but the Parthenon is mind-blowing—and then to Ephesus in Turkey, where they have these ancient public lavatories in marble with a place in the middle for musicians to serenade." When they arrived in Istanbul, he hired a history professor to give them a tour. Finally, they proceeded to a Turkish bath, where the professor's talk provided Jobs with an insight into youth globalisation: "I had a real revelation." We were all dressed in robes, and they served us Turkish coffee. "So fucking what?" I thought as the professor explained how the coffee was produced differently than anywhere else. Which kids, even in Turkey, care about Turkish coffee? I had been staring at young folks in Istanbul all day. They were all drinking what every other child in the globe was drinking, wearing clothes that looked like they were bought at Gap, and using cell phones. They were treated like children everywhere else. It dawned on me that, for young people today, the entire world is the same. There is no such thing as a Turkish phone or a music player that young people in Turkey would desire that is different from one that young people abroad would want when we are designing things. We've become one world. Jobs had occupied himself after the delight of that sail by starting to design, and then continually modifying, a yacht he said he hoped to build someday. When he fell ill again in 2009, he almost called off the project. "I didn't think I'd be alive when it was finished," he recalled. "But that made me so sad that I decided that working on the design would be fun, and maybe I'll still be alive when it's finished." I'd be furious if I stopped working on the yacht and then survived for another two years. So I've continued."

We returned to his house after our omelettes at the café, and he showed me all of the models and architectural designs. The intended yacht was sleek and minimalist, as expected. The teak decks were absolutely flat and free of frills. The cabin windows were huge panes, practically floor to ceiling, like in an Apple store, and the main living room was constructed with glass walls forty feet long and ten feet high. He had commissioned the chief engineer of the Apple stores to create a special glass that could provide structural support. The boat was already being built by the Dutch bespoke yacht builder Feadship at the time, but Jobs was still tinkering with the design. "I know it's possible that I'll die and leave Laurene with a half-finished boat," he admitted. "However, I must persevere. If I don't, it's an admission that I'm dying."

He and Powell were about to celebrate their twentieth wedding anniversary, and he realised that he had not always been as appreciative of her as she deserved. "I'm very lucky, because you just don't know what you're getting into when you get married," he remarked. "You have a sixth sense about things." I couldn't have done better because Laurene is not only brilliant and beautiful, but she's also a great, nice person." He burst into tears for a little moment. He mentioned his other relationships, particularly Tina Redse, but claimed to have ended up in the appropriate spot. He also considered how self-centred and demanding he might be. "Laurene had to deal with that, as well as my illness," he explained. "I understand that living with me is not a piece of cake."

Among his selfish characteristics was a tendency to forget anniversaries and birthdays. In this situation, though, he decided to organise a surprise. They had married at Yosemite's Ahwahnee Hotel, and he wanted to take Powell back there for their anniversary. However, when Jobs contacted them, the room was already reserved. So he had the hotel contact the individuals who had reserved the suite where he and Powell had stayed and ask them if they would be willing to release it. "I offered to pay for another weekend," Jobs remembered, adding, "and the man was very nice and said, 'Twenty years, please take it, it's yours.'"

He discovered wedding images taken by a friend and had large copies made on thick paper boards and placed in an attractive box. He found the message he had written to include in the package while scrolling through his iPhone and read it aloud: Twenty years ago, we didn't know anything about each other. We were led by our instincts, and you completely swept me off my feet. When we got married at the Ahwahnee, it was snowing. Years passed, children arrived, good times, difficult times, but never horrible moments. Our affection and respect have endured and expanded. We've been through so much together, and here we are, 20 years later, older and wiser, with wrinkles on our faces and hearts. We've experienced many of life's joys, sorrows, secrets, and wonders, and we're still here together. My feet have never touched the ground again. He was sobbing hysterically towards the end of the recitation. When he came to, he realised he had made a set of the images for each of his children. "I figured they'd like to see that I was once young."

In 2001 Jobs had a vision: Your personal computer would serve as a "digital hub" for a variety of lifestyle devices, such as music players, video recorders, phones, and tablets. This played to Apple's strength of creating end-to-end products that were simple to use. The company was thus transformed from a high-end niche computer company to the most valuable technology company in the world.

By 2008 Jobs had developed a vision for the next wave of the digital era. In the future, he believed, your desktop computer would no longer serve as the hub for your content. Instead the hub would move to "the cloud." In other words, your content would be stored on remote servers managed by a company you trusted, and it would be available for you to use on any device, anywhere. It would take him three years to get it right. He began with a false step. In the summer of 2008 he launched a product called MobileMe, an expensive ($99 per year) subscription service that allowed you to store your address book, documents, pictures, videos, email, and calendar remotely in the cloud and to sync them with any device. In theory, you could go to your iPhone or any computer and access all aspects of your digital life. There was, however, a big problem: The service, to use Jobs's terminology, sucked. It was complex, devices didn't sync well, and email and other data got lost randomly in the ether. "Apple's MobileMe Is Far Too Flawed to Be Reliable," was the headline on Walt Mossberg's review in the Wall Street Journal. Jobs was furious. He gathered the MobileMe team in the auditorium on the Apple campus, stood onstage, and asked, "Can anyone tell me what MobileMe is supposed to do?" After the team members offered their answers, Jobs shot back: "So why the fuck doesn't it do that?" Over the next half hour he continued to berate them. "You've tarnished Apple's reputation," he said. "You should hate each other for having let each other down. Mossberg, our friend, is no longer writing good things about us." In front of the whole audience, he got rid of the leader of the MobileMe team and replaced him with Eddy Cue, who oversaw all Internet content at Apple. As Fortune's Adam Lashinsky reported in a dissection of the Apple corporate culture, "Accountability is strictly enforced."

By 2010 it was clear that Google, Amazon, Microsoft, and others were aiming to be the company that could best store all of your content and data in the cloud and sync it on your various devices. So Jobs redoubled his efforts. As he explained it to me that fall: We need to be the company that manages your relationship with the cloud—streams your music and videos from the cloud, stores your pictures and information, and maybe even your medical data. Apple was the first to have the insight about your computer becoming a digital hub. So we wrote all of these apps—iPhoto, iMovie, iTunes—and tied them to our devices, like the iPod, iPhone and iPad, and it worked brilliantly. But over the next few years, the hub is going to move from your computer into the cloud. So it's the same digital hub strategy, but the hub's in a different place. It means you will always have access to your content and you won't have to sync. It's important that we make this transformation, because of what Clayton Christensen calls "the innovator's dilemma," where people who invent something are usually the last ones to see past it, and we certainly don't want to be left behind. I'm going to take MobileMe and make it free, and we're going to make syncing content simple. We are building a server farm in North Carolina. We can provide all the syncing you need, and that way we can lock in the customer. Jobs discussed this vision at his Monday morning meetings, and gradually it was refined to a new strategy. "I sent emails to groups of people at 2 a.m. and batted things around," he recalled. "We think about this a lot because it's not a job, it's our life." Although some board members, including Al Gore, questioned the idea of making MobileMe free, they supported it. It would be their strategy for attracting customers into Apple's orbit for the next decade. The new service was named iCloud, and Jobs unveiled it in his keynote address to Apple's Worldwide Developers Conference in June 2011. He was still on medical leave and, for some days in May, had been hospitalised with infections and pain. Some close friends urged him not to make the presentation, which would involve lots of preparation and rehearsals. But the prospect of ushering in another tectonic shift in the digital age seemed to energise him. He was wearing a VON ROSEN black cashmere sweater over his normal Issey Miyake black turtleneck and thermal underwear beneath his blue trousers when he took the stage at the San Francisco Convention Center. But he appeared thinner than ever. The audience gave him a long standing ovation—"That always helps, and I appreciate it," he said—but Apple's stock sank more than $4, to $340, within minutes. He was making a valiant effort, but he appeared frail. He gave the stage to Phil Schiller and Scott Forstall to demonstrate the new operating systems for Macs and mobile devices, then returned to demonstrate iCloud. "About ten years ago, we had one of our most important insights," he remarked. "The PC was going to be the centre of your digital life." Your films, photos, and music. However, it has recently broken down. Why?" He remarked on how difficult it was to get all of your content synced to all of your devices. If you have music on your iPad, a photo on your iPhone, and a video on your PC, you may find yourself feeling like an old-fashioned switchboard operator as you plug USB connections into and out of items to get the information shared. "Keeping these devices in sync is driving us crazy," he laughed. "We've got a solution. It's our next great revelation. We are relegating the PC and Mac to the status of a device, and we are moving the digital hub to the cloud."

Jobs was well aware that his "big insight" was not truly novel. Indeed, he made a joke about Apple's prior attempt, saying, "You may wonder, Why should I believe them? They're the ones who introduced me to MobileMe." The audience nervously laughed. "Let me just say that it wasn't our finest hour." However, as he demonstrated iCloud, it was obvious that it would be superior. Mail, contacts, and calendar items were promptly synced. Apps, photographs, books, and documents all followed suit. Most notably, Jobs and Eddy Cue had struck relationships with record labels (unlike Google and Amazon). Apple's cloud servers would hold eighteen million songs. If you possessed any of these on any of your devices or computers, whether legally purchased or pirated, Apple would allow you to access a high-quality version of it on all of your devices without having to upload it to the cloud. "It just all works," he added. As always, Apple's competitive advantage was the simple premise that everything would just function flawlessly. Microsoft had been promoting "Cloud Power" for more than a year, and three years earlier, the legendary Ray Ozzie, the company's chief software architect, had issued a rallying cry: "Our aspiration is that individuals will only need to licence their media once, and use any of their... devices to access and enjoy their media." However, Ozzie left Microsoft at the end of 2010, and the company's cloud computing effort never materialised in consumer devices. In 2011, both Amazon and Google offered cloud services, but none had the ability to combine the hardware, software, and content of a range of devices. Apple owned and designed every link in the chain, including the devices, computers, operating systems, and application software, as well as the selling and storage of content. Of course, it only worked provided you used an Apple device and stayed within Apple's guarded yard. This resulted in another benefit for Apple: client loyalty. It would be difficult to convert to a Kindle or Android device if you started using iCloud. Your music and other content would not sync with them; in fact, they may not operate at all. It was the result of three decades of avoiding open systems. "We considered doing a music client for Android," Jobs told me over breakfast the next morning. "We put iTunes on Windows so that we could sell more iPods." But, aside from making Android users happy, I don't see any benefit to having our music app on Android. And I don't want to please Android users."

Jobs had sought up Bill Hewlett in the phone directory when he was thirteen, contacted him to score a part he needed for a frequency counter he was attempting to make, and ended up earning a summer job at Hewlett-Packard's instruments business. The following year, HP purchased some land in Cupertino to grow its calculator branch. Wozniak went to work there, and it was during his spare time that he invented the Apple I and Apple II. When HP chose to close its Cupertino campus in 2010, which was roughly a mile east of Apple's One Infinite Loop headquarters, Jobs discreetly agreed to buy it and the adjacent property. He appreciated the way Hewlett-Packard had developed a long-lasting corporation, and he was proud to have done the same at Apple. Now he desired a showpiece headquarters, something that no West Coast technology firm possessed. He finally bought 150 acres, much of which had previously been apricot orchards, and plunged himself into what would become a legacy project that blended his passion for design with his enthusiasm for building an enduring firm. "I want to leave a signature campus that expresses the values of the company for future generations," he stated.

He chose Sir Norman Foster's architectural firm, who had done cleverly engineered buildings such as the rebuilt Reichstag in Berlin and 30 St. Mary Axe in London, which he believed to be the best in the world. Not surprisingly, Jobs became so involved in the planning, both the concept and the specifics, that reaching a final design became nearly impossible. This was to be his final structure, and he wanted it to be perfect. Foster's firm allocated fifty architects to the project, and they gave Jobs revised models and ideas every three weeks throughout 2010. He would repeatedly come up with fresh notions, sometimes totally new shapes, and force them to restart and present more options. The building was formed like a gigantic winding racetrack consisting of three linked semi circles around a large central courtyard when he first showed me the models and drawings in his living room. The interior contained rows of office pods that enabled sunlight to flood down the aisles, and the walls were floor-to-ceiling glass. "It allows for chance and fluid meeting spaces," he says, "and everyone gets to participate in the sunlight."

A month later, he showed me the designs in Apple's enormous conference room across from his office, where a model of the proposed building filled the table. He'd made a significant change. The pods would all be situated back from the windows, allowing vast passageways to be illuminated. These would also function as common areas. Some of the architects argued that the windows should be able to be opened. Jobs disliked the concept of others being able to open things. "That would just allow people to screw things up," he said. He won on this, as well as other points. Jobs showed up the drawings at dinner that night, and Reed remarked that the overhead view reminded him of male genitalia. His father rejected the remark as typical of a teen's mindset. However, the following day, he mentioned the remark to the architects. "Unfortunately, once I've told you that, you're never going to be able to erase that image from your mind," he explained. The shape had been modified to a basic circle by the time I returned. Because of the revised design, there would be no straight pieces of glass in the building. Everything would be curved and connected together effortlessly. Jobs had long been interested in glass, and his experience requiring gigantic custom panes for Apple's retail locations gave him confidence that massive curved pieces could be produced in large quantities. He showed me the intended middle courtyard, which was 800 feet across (more than three average city blocks, or nearly the length of three football fields), with overlays demonstrating how it could surround St. Peter's Square in Rome. One of his lingering memories was of the orchards that had dominated the area, so he hired a senior arborist from Stanford and declared that 80% of the acreage would be landscaped naturally, with 6,000 trees. "I asked him to make sure to include a new set of apricot orchards," Jobs said. "You used to see them everywhere, even on the corners, and they're part of the legacy of this valley."

The plans for the four-story, three-million-square-foot facility, which would house over a thousand employees, were ready to be unveiled in June 2011. He made the decision in a low-key and unnoticed presentation before the Cupertino City Council the day after announcing iCloud at the Worldwide Developers Conference.

Despite his lack of energy, he had a full day planned. Ron Johnson, who had built and overseen Apple's stores for more than a decade, had decided to accept an offer to become CEO of J.C. Penney, and he stopped by Jobs' residence in the morning to discuss his departure. Then Jobs and I proceeded to Fraiche, a little yoghurt and oatmeal café in Palo Alto, where he chatted animatedly about potential future Apple goods. Later that day, he was taken to Santa Clara for Apple's quarterly meeting with top Intel executives, during which they discussed the use of Intel chips in future mobile devices. Jobs had pondered attending U2's performance at the Oakland Coliseum that night. Instead, he chose that evening to present his intentions to the Cupertino City Council. He arrived without an entourage or any fuss, looking casual in the same black sweater he wore for his developers conference speech, and stood on a podium with a clicker in hand, exhibiting slides of the design to council members for twenty minutes. He paused and smiled as a rendering of the sleek, futuristic, completely circular edifice flashed on the screen. "It's almost like a spaceship has landed," he remarked. He then said, "I think we have a shot at building the best office building in the world."

The following Friday, Jobs sent an email to a former colleague, Ann Bowers, the widow of Intel pioneer Bob Noyce. In the early 1980s, she was Apple's human resources director and den mother, responsible for reprimanding Jobs after his outbursts and caring for his coworkers' wounds. Jobs invited her to come see him the next day. Bowers was in New York at the time, but she stopped by his residence when she returned on Sunday. He was unwell again by then, in pain and lacking energy, but he was eager to show her the renderings of the new headquarters. "You should be proud of Apple," he told her. "You should be proud of what we have built."

Then he glanced at her and asked her a question that nearly knocked her off her feet: "Tell me, what was I like when I was young?"

Bowers tried to be truthful with him. "You were very impetuous and difficult," she responded. "However, your vision was intriguing. You once said to us, 'The journey is the reward.' That proved to be correct."

"Yes," Jobs replied. "I did learn some things along the way." He then repeated it a few minutes later, as if to reassure Bowers and himself. "I learned a few things." I truly did."

CHAPTER 27

ROUND THREE

Jobs had a burning desire to attend his son's high school graduation in June 2010. "When I was diagnosed with cancer, I made my deal with God or whatever, which was that I really wanted to see Reed graduate, and that got me through 2009," he explained. Reed, as a senior, resembled his father at the age of eighteen, with a knowing and slightly rebellious smile, intense eyes, and a shock of dark hair. But he inherited from his mother a sweetness and excruciatingly sensitive empathy that his father lacked. He exuded affection and a desire to please. When his father sat sullenly at the kitchen table, staring at the floor, as he often did when he was sick, the only thing that could make his eyes sparkle was Reed strolling in. Reed was devoted to his father. Soon after I began working on this book, he dropped by where I was staying and suggested we go for a stroll, like his father often did. With a very genuine expression, he told me that his father was not a cold profit-seeking businessman, but was motivated by a love of what he did and pride in the items he was producing. Reed began working in a Stanford oncology lab using DNA sequencing to uncover genetic indicators for colon cancer after Jobs was diagnosed with cancer. In one investigation, he followed mutations through families. "One of the few silver linings of my illness is that Reed has had the opportunity to study with some very good doctors," Jobs stated. "I remember how excited I was about computers when I was his age." The convergence of biology and technology, I believe, will be the most significant inventions of the twenty-first century. A new era has begun, just as the digital era did when I was his age."

Reed's cancer research served as the foundation for his senior report, which he delivered to his Crystal Springs Uplands School class. His father, along with the rest of his family, sat in the audience, grinning, as he detailed how he utilised centrifuges and dyes to sequence the DNA of tumours. "I fantasise about Reed getting a house here in

Palo Alto with his family and riding his bike to work as a doctor at Stanford," Jobs explained later. Reed had matured quickly in 2009, when his father appeared to be dying. While his parents were in Memphis, he looked after his younger sisters and acquired a protective paternalism. However, when his father's health improved in the spring of 2010, he reverted to his lively, taunting demeanour. During dinner one day, he was talking with his family where he should take his fiancée for dinner. His father suggested Il Fornaio, an exquisite Palo Alto restaurant, but Reed stated he couldn't secure reservations. "Do you want me to try?" questioned his father. Reed resisted, preferring to handle the situation himself. Erin, the somewhat shy middle child, suggested that she and Eve, the younger sister, set up a tepee in their garden and serve them a romantic lunch there. Reed rose and hugged her. He agreed to take her up on her offer another time. Reed was one of four candidates on his school's Quiz Kids team who competed on a local TV station one Saturday. The entire family, with the exception of Eve, who was competing in a horse event, came to support him. As the television team fumbled around getting ready, his father tried to keep his frustration in check and blend in with the parents seated in the rows of folding chairs. But he was easily identified in his signature trousers and black turtleneck, and one woman took up a chair right close to him and began photographing him. He rose up and proceeded to the other end of the row without looking at her. When Reed arrived on site, his nameplate read "Reed Powell." The host inquired as to what the students wished to be when they grew up. "A cancer researcher," Reed replied.

Jobs drove Reed in his two-seat Mercedes SL55, while his wife followed in her own car with Erin. She questioned Erin on the drive home why she felt her father refused to have a licence plate on his automobile. "To be a rebel," she explained. I later asked Jobs the question. "Because people follow me sometimes, and if I have a licence plate, they can track down where I live," he explained. "However, with Google Maps, that's kind of becoming obsolete." So, I think it's just because I don't."

During Reed's graduation ceremony, his father texted me from his iPhone, simply saying, "Today is one of my happiest days." Reed is about to graduate from high school. At the moment. And, despite all odds, I'm here." That night, they hosted a party for close friends and family. Reed danced with his entire family, including his father. Later, Jobs took his son out to the barn-style storage shed and offered him one of his two bicycles, which he would never ride again. When Reed remarked that the Italian one appeared a little too gay, Jobs advised him to select the sturdy eight-speed next to it. When Reed mentioned being owed, Jobs responded, "You don't need to be indebted because you have my DNA." Toy Story 3 was released a few days later. Jobs had cultivated this Pixar trilogy since its inception, and the final piece dealt with Andy's leaving for college. "I wish I could always be with you," says Andy's mother. "You will always be," he says.

Erin, his middle daughter, had grown into a poised and lovely young woman with a more mature personal sensitivity than her father. She considered becoming an architect, possibly because of her father's interest in the field, and she had an excellent sense of design.

Powell told me that Erin wanted to interview me while I was finishing this book. I wouldn't have asked for it because she was just sixteen at the time, but I agreed. Erin highlighted that she knew why her father wasn't always attentive and that she accepted it. "He does his best to be both a father and the CEO of Apple, and he juggles those pretty well," she explained. "I wish I had more of his attention at times, but I know the work he's doing is critical and I think it's really cool, so I'm fine." I don't think I need any more attention."

Jobs had vowed to take each of his children on a journey of their choosing when they reached the age of adolescence. Reed chose Kyoto because he knew how much his father was captivated by the Zen tranquillity of that wonderful city. Not surprisingly, Erin chose Kyoto as her thirteenth birthday destination in 2008. Because of her father's illness, he had to cancel the vacation, but he vowed to take her in 2010, when he was feeling better. But he changed his mind in June and decided not to go. Erin was disappointed but did not object. Instead, her mother took her to France with family friends, and the Kyoto trip was rescheduled for July. The entire family set off in early July for Kona Village, Hawaii, for the first phase of the journey. However, while in Hawaii, Jobs suffered a severe toothache that he ignored, as if he could will the cavity away. The tooth had collapsed and needed to be repaired. Then the iPhone 4 antenna problem struck, and he decided to return to Cupertino with Reed. Powell and Erin remained in Hawaii, anticipating that Jobs would return and carry out their plans to travel to Kyoto. Jobs did it. While Reed looked after Eve in Palo Alto, Erin and her parents stayed at the Tawaraya Ryokan, a sublimely simple inn that Jobs adored. "It was fantastic," Erin said of the experience.

Jobs had taken Erin's half-sister, Lisa Brennan-Jobs, to Japan when she was around the same age. Sharing delicious meals with him and watching him devour unagi sushi and other delights were among her favourite memories. Lisa felt at ease with him for the first time after seeing him enjoy his food. "Dad knew exactly where he wanted to go for lunch every day," Erin recounted. He told me he knew an outstanding soba shop and took me there; it was so good that I've struggled to eat soba again since nothing compares." They also discovered a little neighbourhood sushi restaurant, which Jobs marked on his iPhone as the "best sushi I've ever had." Erin concurred.

They also went to some of Kyoto's famed Zen Buddhist temples, including Saiho-ji, known as the "moss temple" because of its Golden Pond surrounded by gardens with over a hundred different types of moss. "Erin was really happy, which was deeply gratifying and helped improve her relationship with her father," Powell recounted. "She deserved that."

Eve, their younger daughter, was feisty, self-assured, and unfazed by her father. Her passion was horseback riding, and she resolved to compete in the Olympics. "Tell me exactly what I need to do," she said when a coach told her how much work would be required. "I'll do it." He did, and she began following the regimen religiously. Eve was excellent at the arduous process of locating her father; she frequently called his aide at work directly to ensure that anything was added to his calendar. She was also an excellent negotiator. When the family planned a trip one weekend in 2010, Erin wanted to delay the departure by half a day but was frightened to approach her father. Eve, aged twelve, offered to take on the assignment, and after dinner she presented the case to her father as if she were a Supreme Court lawyer. Jobs cut her off—"No, I don't think I want to"—but he was clearly amused rather than upset. Later that evening, Eve sat down with her mother and discussed the different ways she could have improved her case. Jobs grew to admire her spirit and saw a lot of himself in her. "She's a pistol, and she has the strongest will of any kid I've ever met," he remarked. "It's like payback." He had a strong knowledge of her personality, possibly because it resembled his. "Eve is more sensitive than a lot of people think," he said. "She's so smart that she can kind of roll over people, which means she can alienate people and end up alone." She's learning how to be herself, but she tempers it around the edges so she may have the friends she needs."

Jobs' marriage to his wife was hard at times, but always devoted. Laurene Powell, astute and empathetic, was a calming influence and an example of his ability to compensate for some of his selfish inclinations by surrounding himself with strong-willed and rational people. She spoke calmly on business problems, firmly on family concerns, and vehemently on medical issues. She co-founded and established College Track, a national after-school program that assists poor students in graduating from high school and enrolling in college, early in their marriage. She has since been a driving influence in the education reform movement. Despite his typical disdain for charity activities, Jobs expressed praise for his wife's work: "What she's done with College Track really impresses me."

Jobs celebrated his fifty-fifth birthday with his family in February 2010. His kids got him a red-velvet toy crown to wear, and the kitchen was decked with streamers and balloons. He resumed his emphasis on his career after recovering from a tough year of health problems. "I think it was hard on the family, especially the girls," she admitted. "After two years of being ill, he finally gets better, and they expected him to focus a little more on them, but he didn't." She wanted to make sure that both sides of his personality were represented and contextualised in this book, she explained. "Like many great men whose gifts are extraordinary, he's not extraordinary in every realm," she explained. "He lacks social graces, such as putting himself in other people's shoes, but he is deeply committed to empowering humanity, advancing humanity, and putting the right tools in their hands."

Powell visited Washington in the early fall of 2010 and talked with several of her White House contacts, who informed her that President Obama would be visiting Silicon Valley that October. He might want to meet with her husband, she offered. Obama's advisers loved the concept because it aligned with his new emphasis on competition. Furthermore, John Doerr, a venture capitalist and personal friend of Jobs', spoke at a meeting of the President's Economic Recovery Advisory Board regarding Jobs' views on why the United States was losing its advantage. He, too, proposed that Obama meet with Jobs. So a half-hour session at the Westin San Francisco Airport was added to the president's agenda.

The only issue was that when Powell told her husband, he stated he didn't want to do it. He was irritated because she had done it behind his back. "I'm not going to get slotted in for a token meeting just so he can check off that he met with a CEO," he said. Obama, she said, was "really psyched to meet with you." Jobs responded that if such were the case, Obama should personally call and request the meeting. The stalemate lasted five days. Jobs eventually gave up.

The meeting lasted 45 minutes in total, and Jobs did not hold back. "You're headed for a one-term presidency," Jobs warned Obama from the start. To avoid this, he stated that the administration needs to be far more business-friendly. He emphasised how simple it was to create a factory in China and how difficult it was to do it in America these days, owing to restrictions and excessive fees. Jobs also blasted America's educational system, claiming that it was hopelessly outdated and hampered by union labour rules. There was almost little prospect for school reform until the teachers' unions were shattered. Teachers, he believes, should be treated as professionals rather than as assembly-line workers. Principals should be able to hire and terminate employees depending on their performance. Schools should be open until at least 6 p.m., and they should be in session eleven months of the year. He thought it was preposterous that American classrooms still relied on teachers standing at a chalkboard and using textbooks. All books, learning materials, and tests should be digital and interactive, personalised for each student, and provide real-time feedback. Jobs volunteered to put together a group of six or seven CEOs who could truly explain America's innovation issues, and the president agreed. So Jobs compiled a list of folks for a December meeting in Washington. Unfortunately, after Valerie Jarrett and other presidential aides supplied names, the list had grown to around twenty people, with GE's Jeffrey Immelt leading the pack. Jobs informed Jarrett that the list was bloated and that he had no intention of attending. In truth, his health issues had flared up again by then, and he would not have been able to go anyhow, as Doerr privately explained to the president. Doerr began planning a small dinner for President Obama in Silicon Valley in February 2011. He and Jobs travelled to Evvia, a Greek restaurant in Palo Alto, with their spouses to finalise the guest list. Google's Eric Schmidt, Yahoo's Carol Bartz, Facebook's Mark Zuckerberg, Cisco's John Chambers, Oracle's Larry Ellison, Genentech's Art Levinson, and Netflix's Reed Hastings were among the dozen chosen tech titans. Jobs' attention to the finer points of the meal extended to the cuisine. Doerr handed him the proposed menu, and he replied that some of the dishes—shrimp, cod, lentil salad—were simply too fancy "and not who you are, John." He was especially upset about the dessert, a cream pie topped with chocolate truffles, but the White House advance staff overruled him by assuring the caterer that the president preferred cream pie. Doerr kept the house so warm since Jobs had lost so much weight that he was so easily chilly that Zuckerberg found himself sweating heavily. Jobs began the event by declaring, "Regardless of our political persuasions, I want you to know that we're here to do whatever you ask to help our country." Despite this, the event quickly devolved into a series of proposals for what the president should do to help the local businesses. Chambers, for example, advocated for a repatriation tax holiday, which would allow significant firms to avoid paying taxes on overseas profits if they brought them back to the US for investment during a specific time period. The president was irritated, as was Zuckerberg, who leaned to his right and whispered, "We should be talking about what's important to the country." "How come he's only talking about what's good for him?"

Doerr was able to refocus the discussion by asking everyone to contribute ideas for action items. When it was Jobs' turn, he emphasised the need for more qualified engineers and proposed that any foreign students who received an engineering degree in the United States be granted a visa to remain in the nation. Obama stated that this could only be done in the framework of the "Dream Act," which would allow illegal aliens who entered as youngsters and completed high school to become legal residents—something Republicans have resisted. Jobs found this to be a vexing example of how politics can paralyse. "The president is very intelligent, but he kept explaining to us why things couldn't be done," he recounted. "It infuriates me."

Jobs then urged that a method be discovered to teach more American engineers. He claimed that Apple employed 700,000 industrial workers in China because it required 30,000 engineers on-site to support those people. "You can't find that many in America to hire," he explained. These factory engineers did not need to be PhDs or geniuses; they only needed fundamental industrial engineering skills. They could be trained in technical schools, community colleges, or trade schools. "If you could educate these engineers," he suggested, "we could move more manufacturing plants here." The president was very moved by the argument. He told his advisers two or three times over the next month, "We've got to find ways to train those 30,000 manufacturing engineers that Jobs told us about."

Jobs was thrilled that Obama followed up, and they spoke several times by phone after the meeting. He offered to assist in the creation of Obama's political advertisements for the 2012 campaign. (He'd made the same offer in 2008, but was irritated when Obama's adviser David Axelrod wasn't completely subservient.) "I believe that political advertising is horrible. "I'd like to bring Lee Clow out of retirement, and we can come up with great commercials for him," Jobs told me a few weeks later. Jobs had been fighting pain all week, but political discourse rejuvenated him. "Every now and then, a true advertising pro gets involved, as Hal Riney did with 'It's Morning in America' for Reagan's reelection in 1984." That is what I would like to accomplish for Obama."

When the cancer resurfaced, it always gave signs. Jobs had discovered this. He'd lose his appetite and start feeling pains all over his body. His physicians would run tests, find nothing, and convince him that he was fine. But he was wiser. The cancer developed its own signalling channels, and a few months after he noticed them, doctors discovered that it was no longer in remission. In early November 2010, another such decline occurred. He was in discomfort, had stopped eating, and required intravenous feeding by a nurse who came to the house. The physicians detected no evidence of new tumours and concluded that this was just another of his regular bouts with infections and stomach problems. He had never been one to suffer in silence, so his doctors and family had become accustomed to his complaints.

He and his family spent Thanksgiving in Kona Village, but his eating habits did not improve. The meals were served in a shared room, and the other guests pretended not to notice while Jobs, who appeared emaciated, rocked and groaned during meals, not touching his food. It was a credit to the resort and its guests that his condition was never made public. When Jobs returned to Palo Alto, he became more emotional and depressed. He informed his children that he feared he was going to die, and he would get emotional thinking about how he would never be able to celebrate any of their birthdays again. He got down to 115 pounds by Christmas, which was more than fifty pounds below his typical weight. Mona Simpson, her ex-husband, television comedy writer Richard Appel, and their children spent the holidays in Palo Alto. The mood improved slightly. For a while, the families played parlour games like Novel, in which participants strive to trick one another by writing the most convincing fake beginning sentence of a book, and things looked to be looking up. A few days after Christmas, he was even able to go out to dinner with Powell. For New Year's, the kids went skiing, with Powell and Mona Simpson taking turns staying at home with Jobs in Palo Alto.

However, by the beginning of 2011, it was evident that this was not a one-time blip. His doctors discovered additional tumours, and the cancer-related signals aggravated his appetite loss. They were trying to figure out how much pharmacological therapy his body could tolerate in its weakened state. As he moaned and slumped over in pain, he told them that every inch of his body felt like it had been punched. It was a never-ending cycle. The early signals of cancer were painful. His appetite was suppressed by the morphine and other medications he was taking. Because his pancreas had been removed in part and his liver had been replaced, his digestive system was defective and he had difficulty digesting protein. Losing weight makes it more difficult to begin aggressive pharmacological therapy. His malnourished state, as well as the immunosuppressants he used to keep his body from rejecting his liver transplant, made him more susceptible to infections. Weight reduction weakened the lipid layers around his pain receptors, exacerbating his discomfort. He was also prone to dramatic mood swings, characterised by protracted periods of rage and melancholy, which further restricted his appetite.

Jobs' eating difficulties were aggravated over time by his psychological relationship with food. When he was younger, he discovered that fasting might cause euphoria and ecstasy. So, even though he knew he should eat—his physicians were pleading with him to consume high-quality protein—he revealed that his propensity for fasting and diets like Arnold Ehret's fruit regimen, which he had embraced as a youngster, lingered in the back of his subconscious. Powell kept telling him he was crazy, even pointing out that Ehret had died at the age of fifty-six when he stumbled and smacked his skull, and she would get irritated when he came to the table and just stared blankly at his lap. "I wanted him to force himself to eat," she explained, "and it was incredibly tense at home." Bryar Brown, their part-time cook, would still come in the afternoon and prepare a variety of healthful foods, but Jobs would try one or two and then trash them all as unpalatable. "I could probably eat a little pumpkin pie," he said one evening, and the even-tempered Brown made a magnificent pie from scratch in an hour. Jobs only ate one bite, but Brown was overjoyed. When the cancer resurfaced, it always gave signs. Jobs had discovered this. He'd lose his appetite and start feeling pains all over his body. His physicians would run tests, find nothing, and convince him that he was fine. But he was wiser. The cancer developed its own signalling channels, and a few months after he noticed them, doctors discovered that it was no longer in remission.

In early November 2010, another such decline occurred. He was in discomfort, had stopped eating, and required intravenous feeding by a nurse who came to the house. The physicians detected no evidence of new tumours and concluded that this was just another of his regular bouts with infections and stomach problems. He had never been one to suffer in silence, so his doctors and family had become accustomed to his complaints.

He and his family spent Thanksgiving in Kona Village, but his eating habits did not improve. The meals were served in a shared room, and the other guests pretended not to notice while Jobs, who appeared emaciated, rocked and groaned during meals, not touching his food. It was a credit to the resort and its guests that his condition was never made public. When Jobs returned to Palo Alto, he became more emotional and depressed. He informed his children that he feared he was going to die, and he would get emotional thinking about how he would never be able to celebrate any of their birthdays again.

He got down to 115 pounds by Christmas, which was more than fifty pounds below his typical weight. Mona Simpson, her ex-husband, television comedy writer Richard Appel, and their children spent the holidays in Palo Alto. The mood improved slightly. For a while, the families played parlour games like Novel, in which participants strive to trick one another by writing the most convincing fake beginning sentence of a book, and things looked to be looking up. A few days after Christmas, he was even able to go out to dinner with Powell. For New Year's, the kids went skiing, with Powell and Mona Simpson taking turns staying at home with Jobs in Palo Alto.

However, by the beginning of 2011, it was evident that this was not a one-time blip. His doctors discovered additional tumours, and the cancer-related signals aggravated his appetite loss. They were trying to figure out how much pharmacological therapy his body could tolerate in its weakened state. As he moaned and slumped over in pain, he told them that every inch of his body felt like it had been punched. It was a never-ending cycle. The early signals of cancer were painful. His appetite was suppressed by the morphine and other medications he was taking. Because his pancreas had been removed in part and his liver had been replaced, his digestive system was defective and he had difficulty digesting protein. Losing weight makes it more difficult to begin aggressive pharmacological therapy. His malnourished state, as well as the immunosuppressants he used to keep his body from rejecting his liver transplant, made him more susceptible to infections. Weight reduction weakened the lipid layers around his pain receptors, exacerbating his discomfort. He was also prone to dramatic mood swings, characterised by protracted periods of rage and melancholy, which further restricted his appetite.

Jobs' eating difficulties were aggravated over time by his psychological relationship with food. When he was younger, he discovered that fasting might cause euphoria and ecstasy. So, even though he knew he should eat—his physicians were pleading with him to consume high-quality protein—he revealed that his propensity for fasting and diets like Arnold Ehret's fruit regimen, which he had embraced as a youngster, lingered in the back of his subconscious. Powell kept telling him he was crazy, even pointing out that Ehret had died at the age of fifty-six when he stumbled and smacked his skull, and she would get irritated when he came to the table and just stared blankly at his lap. "I wanted him to force himself to eat," she explained, "and it was incredibly tense at home." Bryar Brown, their part-time cook, would still come in the afternoon and prepare a variety of healthful foods, but Jobs would try one or two and then trash them all as unpalatable. "I could probably eat a little pumpkin pie," he said one evening, and the even-tempered Brown made a magnificent pie from scratch in an hour. Jobs only ate one bite, but Brown was overjoyed. Despite Powell's rigorous oversight of her husband's care, he was the one who made the final decision on each new treatment regimen. A classic incident occurred in May 2011, when he met with George Fisher and other Stanford doctors, the Broad Institute's gene-sequencing experts, and his outside consultant David Agus. They were all seated at a table in a suite at the Four Seasons hotel in Palo Alto. Powell did not show up, but Reed, their son, did. For three hours, Stanford and Broad experts presented new information on the genetic fingerprints of his disease that they had discovered. Jobs was his usual obstinate self. At one occasion, he halted a Broad Institute analyst who was using PowerPoint slides incorrectly. Jobs chastised him and explained why Apple's Keynote presentation software was superior; he even offered to train him in its use. By the end of the meeting, Jobs and his team had reviewed all of the molecular data, evaluated the rationales for each of the prospective medicines, and developed a list of tests to assist them rank these.

One of his doctors told him that there was a chance that his cancer, and others like it, might eventually be regarded as a treatable chronic disease that could be managed until the patient died of something else. "I'm either going to be one of the first to be able to outrun a cancer like this, or I'm going to be one of the last to die from it," Jobs said after one of his doctor's appointments. "Either among the first to reach shore or among the last to be dumped."

When his medical absence was revealed in 2011, the situation appeared to be so serious that Lisa Brennan-Jobs contacted him after more than a year and arranged for him to fly from New York the next week. Her father's connection with her had been built on resentment. She was understandably damaged by his abandonment of her for the first ten years of her life. To make matters worse, she had inherited some of his prickliness as well as part of her mother's feeling of resentment. "I told her many times that I wished I'd been a better dad when she was five, but she should let things go now rather than be angry for the rest of her life," he recalled just before Lisa arrived.

The visit went smoothly. Jobs was starting to feel better, and he was in the mood to heal ties and demonstrate his love for people around him. Lisa was in a meaningful relationship for the first time in her life at the age of 32. Her lover was a struggling young filmmaker from California, and Jobs even suggested that if they married, she return to Palo Alto. "Look, I don't know how long I'll be in this world," he admitted. "The physicians are unable to tell me. You'll have to move out here if you want to see more of me. Why don't you think about it?" Despite the fact that Lisa did not relocate west, Jobs was satisfied with how the reconciliation had turned out. "I wasn't sure I wanted her to come because I was sick and didn't want any more complications." But I'm delighted she showed up. It helped me sort out a lot of issues."

That month, Jobs received another visit from someone who wanted to mend fences. Larry Page, Google's co founder who lived less than three blocks away, had just revealed ambitions to seize the company's helm from Eric Schmidt. He understood how to compliment Jobs: he asked if he may stop by and pick up some pointers on how to be a good CEO. Jobs remained enraged about Google. "My first thought was, 'Fuck you,'" he said. "But then I thought about it and realised that everyone, from Bill Hewlett to the guy down the block who worked for HP, helped me when I was young." So I returned his call and answered, "Sure." Page came over, sat in Jobs' living room, and listened to his thoughts on creating excellent products and long-lasting businesses. Jobs remembered, "We talked a lot about focus." And selecting people. How to recognize who to trust and how to assemble a reliable team of lieutenants. I outlined the blocking and tackling he'd have to undertake to protect the team from being flabby or overrun with B players. I emphasised the need for concentration. Determine what Google wishes to be when it grows up. It is now all over the place. What are the five products on which you want to concentrate your efforts? Get rid of the rest since they are holding you back. They are transforming you into Microsoft. They are driving you to produce items that are adequate but not excellent. I attempted to be as helpful as possible. That is something I will continue to do with folks like Mark Zuckerberg. That's how I'm planning to spend some of my remaining time. I can help the next generation remember the great companies that have come before them and how to carry on the history. The Valley has been quite encouraging. I should do everything in my power to repay. Others made a journey to Jobs' Palo Alto home after hearing of his medical leave in 2011. Bill Clinton, for example, stopped by and discussed topics ranging from the Middle East to American politics. But the most moving visit came from the other 1955 tech prodigy, the man who had been Jobs' opponent and collaborator in defining the age of personal computers for more than three decades. Bill Gates has never lost interest in Jobs. In the spring of 2011, I met him at a dinner in Washington, DC, where he had come to discuss his foundation's global health initiatives. He was astounded by the iPad's popularity and how, even while ill, Jobs was working on ways to improve it. "Here I am, merely saving the world from malaria and that sort of thing, and Steve is still coming up with amazing new products," he longingly lamented. "Perhaps I should've stayed in that game." He smiled to let me know he was joking, or at least half-joking.

Gates made plans to visit Jobs in May through their mutual buddy Mike Slade. Jobs's aide called the day before the event to say he wasn't feeling well enough. But it was rescheduled, and Gates drove to Jobs' house early one day, strolled through the back gate to the open kitchen door, and spotted Eve studying at the table. "Is Steve still around?" he inquired. Eve indicated the living room.

They spent more than three hours reminiscing, just the two of them. "We were like the industry's old guys looking back," Jobs remarked. "He was the happiest I'd ever seen him, and I couldn't believe how healthy he looked." Gates was also struck by Jobs's vigour, despite his frighteningly thin appearance. He was frank about his health issues and, for the time being, optimistic. His sequential regimens of targeted pharmacological therapies, he told Gates, were like "jumping from one lily pad to another," as he attempted to keep one step ahead of the cancer.

When Jobs asked about education, Gates sketched out his picture of what schools might be like in the future, with students taking lectures and video classes on their own while using classroom time for discussions and problem solving. They concluded that computers had had a relatively small impact on education, significantly less than on other areas of society such as media, medicine, and law. To remedy that, computers and mobile devices, according to Gates, must focus on delivering more individualised courses and offering motivational feedback. They also discussed the joys of family, including how fortunate they were to have nice children and be married to the right ladies. "We laughed about how fortunate it was that he met Laurene, and she's kept him semi-sane, and I met Melinda, and she's kept me semi-sane," Gates said. "We also talked about how difficult it is to be one of our children and how we can deal with that." It was quite personal." Eve, who had previously competed in horse competitions with Gates's daughter Jennifer, stepped in from the kitchen at one point, and Gates asked her which jumping routines she preferred. As their time together came to an end, Gates praised Jobs for "the incredible stuff" he had produced and for saving Apple from the bozos who were going to ruin it in the late 1990s. He even offered an unusual concession. Throughout their careers, they have held opposing views on one of the most fundamental digital issues: whether hardware and software should be closely linked or more open. "I used to believe that the open, horizontal model would prevail," Gates told him. "However, you demonstrated that the integrated, vertical model could also be excellent." Jobs answered with an admission of his own. "Your model worked well, too," he added. They were both correct. Each model had proven to be effective in the area of personal computers, where Macintosh coexisted with a range of Windows machines, and the same was anticipated to be true in the realm of mobile devices. However, after retelling their conversation, Gates added a qualifier: "The integrated approach works well when Steve is at the helm." However, this does not imply that it will win many rounds in the future." After recalling their meeting, Jobs felt compelled to add a disclaimer about Gates: "Of course, his fragmented model worked, but it didn't produce particularly good products." It made inferior items. That was the issue. The major issue. At least in the long run."

"That Day Has Come"

Jobs has numerous additional ideas and enterprises that he wished to pursue. He wants to disrupt the textbook industry and preserve the spines of backpack-wielding students by developing electronic books and curriculum content for the iPad. He was also collaborating with Bill Atkinson, a buddy from the original Macintosh team, on new digital technologies that operated at the pixel level to allow people to snap beautiful photos with their iPhones even in low-light settings. And he aspired to make television sets as simple and lovely as he had made computers, music players, and phones. "I'd like to design an integrated television set that is completely user-friendly," he explained. "It would be seamlessly synced with all of your devices and iCloud." Users would no longer have to wrestle with complicated remote controls for DVD players and cable channels. "It will have the most basic user interface you can imagine." "I finally got it."

By July 2011, however, his disease had spread to his bones and other regions of his body, and his physicians were having difficulty identifying targeted medications to treat it. He was in agony, sleeping irregularly, had little energy, and had ceased working. He and Powell had reserved a sailboat for a family voyage planned for the end of the month, but those arrangements had been cancelled. He ate almost no solid food and spent the majority of his days in his bedroom watching television.

In August, I received a message from him inviting me to come visit. When I arrived at his house in the middle of the morning on a Saturday, he was still sleeping, so I sat in the garden with his wife and kids, surrounded by a profusion of yellow roses and other sorts of daisies, until he sent word that I should come in. He was snuggled up on the bed, dressed in khaki shorts and a white turtleneck. His legs were eerily stick-like, but his smile was easy and his mind was rapid. "We had better hurry, because I have very little energy," he added.

He wanted to show me some of his personal photographs and let me choose a couple for the book. He indicated various drawers in the room because he was too weak to get out of bed, and I gently brought him the images in each. I sat on the bedside and held them up one at a time so he could see them. Some generated stories, while others got only a grunt or a smile. I'd never seen a photograph of his father, Paul Jobs, and was surprised to come upon one of a gorgeous hardscrabble 1950s dad holding a toddler. "Yes, that's him," he confirmed. "You can make use of it." He then pointed to a box near the window that held a photograph of his father fondly looking at him at his wedding. "He was a great man," Jobs gently stated. I whispered something like, "He would have been proud of you." Jobs corrected me, saying, "He was very proud of me."

The photographs seemed to excite him for a time. We talked about what various people from his background, from Tina Redse to Mike Markkula to Bill Gates, thought of him now. I recalled Gates saying after describing his last encounter with Jobs that Apple had demonstrated that the integrated strategy could succeed, but only "when Steve is at the helm." Jobs thought that was ridiculous. "Anyone could make better products that way, not just me," he explained. So I asked him to name another company that produced excellent products by emphasising end-to-end integration. He pondered for a moment, trying to think of an example. "The car companies," he finally admitted, but added, "Or at least they used to."

When we got to talking about the awful situation of the economy and politics, he had a few scathing words regarding the world's lack of strong leadership. "I'm disappointed in Obama," he confessed. "He's having trouble leading because he's afraid to offend or irritate people." He saw what I was thinking and agreed with a small smile, "Yes, that's not a problem I've ever had."

He became silent after two hours, so I got out of bed and began to go. "Wait," he replied, motioning for me to return to my seat. It took him a few moments to find enough stamina to speak. "I had a lot of trepidation about this project," he finally admitted, alluding to his decision to work on this book. "I was really worried."

"Why did you do it?" I questioned.

"I wanted my kids to know about me," he explained. "I wasn't always there for them, and I wanted them to understand why and what I did." Also, when I became ill, I knew that if I died, other people would write about me and they would know nothing. They'd get everything wrong. So I wanted to make sure that someone heard what I was saying."

In two years, he had never inquired about what I was writing or the conclusions I had reached. But suddenly he turned to face me and added, "I know there will be a lot in your book that I won't like." It was more of a question than a statement, and when he looked at me, I nodded, smiled, and stated I was confident that was correct. "That's good," he commented. "Then it won't appear to be an internal book." I'm not going to read it for a bit because I don't want to become angry. If I'm still alive in a year, I might read it." By then, his eyes were closed and his energy had faded, so I softly exited. Jobs' health deteriorated throughout the summer, and he gradually accepted the inevitable: he would not be returning to Apple as CEO. As a result, it was time for him to step down. For weeks, he agonised over the decision, consulting with his wife, Bill Campbell, Jony Ive, and George Riley. "One of the things I wanted to do for Apple was to set an example of how you do a power transfer right," he explained. He made light of all the difficult adjustments that had occurred at the corporation during the previous thirty-five years. "It's always been a drama, like a third-world country," says the author. Part of my ambition has been to create Apple the best company in the world, and an orderly transition is critical to that."

He concluded that the ideal time and place to make the move would be at the company's regularly scheduled August 24 board meeting. He was eager to do it in person rather than by mail or phone, so he had been forcing himself to eat and restore strength. He decided the day before the conference that he could make it there, but he would need the assistance of a wheelchair. It was decided that he would be driven to headquarters and wheeled into the boardroom as quietly as possible.

He arrived shortly before 11 a.m., just as the board members were wrapping up committee reports and other regular business. Most people were aware of what was about to occur. But instead of going immediately to the item on everyone's mind, Tim Cook and Peter Oppenheimer, the chief financial officer, went through the results for the quarter and the expectations for the year ahead. Jobs then softly stated that he had something personal to communicate. Cook asked if he and the other senior managers should leave, and Jobs paused for more than thirty seconds before he decided they should. He began reading aloud from a letter he had dictated and edited over the previous weeks once the room had been empty of all except the six outside directors. "I have always said that if there ever came a day when I could no longer meet my duties and expectations as Apple's CEO, I would be the first to let you know," the letter started. "Unfortunately, that day has come."

The letter was brief, only eight sentences long, and straightforward. In it, he proposed that Cook take over as CEO and volunteered to serve as chairman of the board. "I believe Apple's best and most innovative days are yet to come." And I'm excited to be a part of its success in a new capacity."

There was a long pause. Al Gore was the first to speak, and he outlined Jobs' achievements throughout his time in office. Watching Jobs create Apple was "the most incredible thing I've ever seen in business," according to Mickey Drexler, and Art Levinson complimented Jobs' efforts in ensuring a smooth transition. Campbell said nothing, but the official resolution ceding authority brought tears to his eyes.

Scott Forstall and Phil Schiller stopped in at lunch to show off mock-ups of some of Apple's upcoming goods. Jobs peppered them with questions and ideas, particularly concerning the capabilities of fourth-generation cellular networks and the features that will be required in future phones. Forstall demonstrated a voice recognition program at one point. Jobs, as he had predicted, snatched the phone in the middle of the demonstration and began to see if he could confuse it. "What's the weather like in Palo Alto?" he inquired. The app responded. After a few more questions, Jobs posed the following question: "Are you a man or a woman?" Surprisingly, the app responded in robotic voice, "They did not assign me a gender." For a little moment, the mood improved.

When the conversation went to tablet computing, some expressed relief that HP had abruptly abandoned the industry, unable to compete with the iPad. But Jobs became solemn and remarked that it was a sad occasion. "Hewlett-Packard built a great company, and they thought they had left it in good hands," he explained. "However, it is now being dismembered and destroyed." It's heartbreaking. I hope I've left a stronger legacy so that this doesn't happen again at Apple." The board members gathered around him as he prepared to leave to offer him a hug. Jobs rode home with George Riley after meeting with his executive team to communicate the news. Powell was in the backyard extracting honey from her hives with the help of Eve when they came. They removed their screen helmets and carried the honey pot to the kitchen, where Reed and Erin had gathered, to celebrate the smooth changeover. Jobs took a spoonful of honey and declared it to be deliciously sweet.

That evening, he told me that he hoped to stay as active as his health would allow. "I'm going to work on new products, marketing, and the things that I like," he stated. When I asked how it felt to leave control of the company he had developed, his tone softened and he changed into the past tense. "I've had a very lucky career, and a very lucky life," he said. "I've done everything I can."

The contents of this book may not be copied, reproduced or transmitted without the express written permission of the author or publisher. Under no circumstances will the publisher or author be responsible or liable for any damages, compensation or monetary loss arising from the information contained in this book, whether directly or indirectly. .

Disclaimer Notice:

Although the author and publisher have made every effort to ensure the accuracy and completeness of the content, they do not, however, make any representations or warranties as to the accuracy, completeness, or reliability of the content. , suitability or availability of the information, products, services or related graphics contained in the book for any purpose. Readers are solely responsible for their use of the information contained in this book

Every effort has been made to make this book possible. If any omission or error has occurred unintentionally, the author and publisher will be happy to acknowledge it in upcoming versions.

Copyright © 2023

All rights reserved.

Printed in Great Britain
by Amazon